Delusions and Beliefs

What sort of mental state is a delusion? What causes delusions? Why are delusions pathological? This book examines these questions, which are normally considered separately, in a much-needed exploration of an important and fascinating topic. Kengo Miyazono assesses the philosophical, psychological, and psychiatric literature on delusions to argue that delusions are malfunctioning beliefs. Delusions belong to the same category as beliefs but – unlike healthy irrational beliefs – fail to play the function of beliefs.

Delusions and Beliefs: A Philosophical Inquiry will be of great interest to students of philosophy of mind and psychology and philosophy of mental disorder, as well as those in related fields such as mental health and psychiatry.

Kengo Miyazono is Associate Professor of Philosophy at Hiroshima University, Japan.

Routledge Focus on Philosophy

Routledge Focus on Philosophy is an exciting and innovative new series, capturing and disseminating some of the best and most exciting new research in philosophy in short book form. Peer reviewed and at a maximum of fifty thousand words shorter than the typical research monograph, *Routledge Focus on Philosophy* titles are available in both ebook and print on demand format. Tackling big topics in a digestible format the series opens up important philosophical research for a wider audience, and as such is invaluable reading for the scholar, researcher and student seeking to keep their finger on the pulse of the discipline. The series also reflects the growing interdisciplinarity within philosophy and will be of interest to those in related disciplines across the humanities and social sciences.

Knowledge Transmission
Stephen Wright

Moral Thinking, Fast and Slow
Hanno Sauer

Political Theory and Global Climate Action
Recasting the Public Sphere
Idil Boran

Delusions and Beliefs
A Philosophical Inquiry
Kengo Miyazono

Extended Consciousness and Predictive Processing
A Third Wave View
Michael D. Kirchhoff and Julian Kiverstein

For more information about this series, please visit: www.routledge.com/Routledge-Focus-on-Philosophy/book-series/RFP

Delusions and Beliefs

A Philosophical Inquiry

Kengo Miyazono

Routledge
Taylor & Francis Group

LONDON AND NEW YORK

First published 2019
by Routledge
4 Park Square, Milton Park, Abingdon, Oxon OX14 4RN
605 Third Avenue, New York, NY 10017

First issued in paperback 2023

Routledge is an imprint of the Taylor & Francis Group, an informa business

British Library Cataloguing-in-Publication Data
A catalogue record for this book is available from the British Library

Library of Congress Cataloging-in-Publication Data
A catalog record for this book has been requested

ISBN: 978-1-03-256998-7 (pbk)
ISBN: 978-1-138-24271-5 (hbk)
ISBN: 978-1-315-27153-8 (ebk)

DOI: 10.4324/9781315271538

Typeset in Times New Roman
by Apex CoVantage, LLC

Publisher's Note
The publisher has gone to great lengths to ensure the quality of this reprint but
points out that some imperfections in the original copies may be apparent.

For Mutsuharu and Tetsuko Yoshida

Contents

Acknowledgments

I am especially grateful to Lisa Bortolotti for her generous support, encouragement, and helpful feedback over the years. I have received invaluable comments and thoughtful criticisms since when I was working on my PhD dissertation, which contains the main ideas of this book. I especially thank Tim Bayne, Alex Byrne, Mathew Broome, Gregory Currie, Daniel Dennett, Richard Dietz, Tamar Gendler, Philip Gerrans, Sung-il Han, Anna Ichino, Masaki Ichinose, Ryan McKay, Ruth Millikan, Yukihiro Nobuhara, John O'Dea, Agustin Rayo, Marga Reimer, Eisuke Sakakibara, and Nick Zangwill.

I also received helpful feedback at the seminars, workshops, and conferences in which I presented my ideas in this book, including PERFECT Reading Group at the University of Birmingham (March 27, 2017); Philosophy, Psychology, and Informatics Group at the University of Edinburgh (March 22, 2017); the 31st International Congress of Psychology at PACIFICO Yokohama, Yokohama (July 26, 2016); Delusions Lunchtime Seminar at the University of Birmingham (June 30, 2015); the 88th Joint Session of the Aristotelian Society and the Mind Association at Cambridge University (July 13, 2014); European Epistemology Research Network Meeting 2014 at Autonomous University of Madrid (June 30, 2014); Functions in the Brain and Brain Mechanisms at the University of Düsseldorf (May 20, 2014); Balzan Workshop: Dreams, Delusion and Early Modern Literature at the University of Birmingham (April 3, 2014); Philosophy of Medicine Seminar at King's College London (February 11, 2014); iCog Inaugural Conference at the University of Sheffield (December 1, 2013); the 2nd PLM Conference at Central European University (September 13, 2013); Philosophy of Psychiatry Work in Progress Day at the University of Lancaster (June 10, 2013); Birmingham Philosophy Society Seminar at the University of Birmingham (March 11, 2013); the First Conference on Contemporary Philosophy in East Asia at Academia Sinica, Taipei (September 8, 2012); the 38th Meeting of Society for Philosophy and Psychology at the University of Colorado at Boulder (June 21, 2012); the 86th Annual Meeting of American Philosophical Association, Pacific Division at Westin Seattle, Seattle, WA (April 6, 2012); Harvard/MIT Friends and Eminees Group at Harvard University (March 6, 2012); the 20th International Meeting of Hongo Metaphysics Club at the University of Tokyo (February 21, 2012); Tim Bayne Lecture Series at the University of Tokyo (February 16, 2012); and the 2011 International Neuroethics Society Annual Meeting at Carnegie Institution for Science, Washington, DC (November 10, 2011).

I thank anonymous reviewers for useful comments and suggestions. I also thank Benjamin Costello for his excellent proofreading.

Chapter 3 is based on my paper 'Delusions as harmful malfunctioning beliefs' (*Consciousness and Cognition*, 2015). Chapter 4 contains some ideas that have been developed through my collaborations with Lisa Bortolotti, Matthew Broome, and Ryan McKay.

This work was supported by JSPS KAKENHI (15J03906, 16H06998, 18H00605).

1 Delusions as malfunctional beliefs

1.1 Overview

A delusion is a belief that is held despite obvious counterevidence and that is not explained by the person's social, cultural, or religious background. Delusions are very often false, and their content can be bizarre. Delusions are typically seen in people with schizophrenia, but they can also be seen in association with a variety of conditions, including dementia, brain injury, drug abuse, etc.[1]

Throughout this book, the term 'delusion' will be used in the clinical sense. The term is also used in the non-clinical sense, typically referring to false or ungrounded ideas, including self-deceptions, daydreams, religious beliefs (e.g., *The God Delusion* (2006) by Richard Dawkins), superstitions, and obsolete scientific theories (e.g., Aristotelian physics). Those non-clinical 'delusions' will not be discussed in this book unless they overlap 'delusions' in the clinical sense (e.g., clinical delusions with religious content).

Delusions are divided into subcategories. A fine-grained distinction is usually made according to the themes or topics of delusions. For example, the delusion of persecution involves the idea of being harmed, harassed, or persecuted by individuals or groups (e.g., 'My colleagues are trying to prevent me from being promoted'). The Capgras delusion involves the idea of a familiar individual being replaced by an imposter (e.g., 'My wife has been replaced by a shape-shifting alien that looks exactly like her'). In addition to the fine-grained distinctions, there are some coarse-grained distinctions. A popular coarse-grained distinction is the one between monothematic and polythematic delusions (Davies et al., 2001; Coltheart, 2013). A monothematic delusion is specific to a particular theme. Polythematic delusions, in contrast, involve more than one theme, often constituting a delusional system. The Capgras delusion is often monothematic,[2] while the delusion of persecution is often polythematic, co-occurring with the delusion of reference (e.g., 'All other passengers of this train are talking about me'), the delusion of grandeur (e.g., 'I have a special power to predict future events'), etc.

Some examples would be useful in order to get a clearer grasp of delusions:

Case 1: the delusion of persecution / the delusion of reference

A Thirty-One-Year-Old Woman with Chronic Schizophrenia. The patient had been ill for seven years. At the time of the interview, she reported olfactory and somatic hallucinations but no auditory or visual hallucinations. She noticed an occasional unexplained powdery smell about her body – something like the smell of baby powder – and was distressed by the experience of physical blows raining down on her head on a daily basis. Marked paranoia was present; she avoided all contact with her family, believing that they would harm her if they knew of her location. She also avoided public places, being generally distrustful of other people. She believed that people followed her with their eyes and gossiped about her whenever she went out in public. The only places that she was prepared to frequent on a relatively regular basis were the gym (at times when other people were unlikely to be present) and a local church that she had started attending.

(Davies et al., 2001, p. 135)

Case 2: the Capgras delusion

DS was a 30-year-old Brazilian man who had been in a coma for three weeks following a head injury (right parietal fracture) sustained in a traffic accident. During the subsequent year, he made remarkable progress in regaining speech, intelligence, and other cognitive skills. He was brought to us by his parents principally because of his tendency to regard them as imposters. When we first saw him he appeared to be an alert and fairly intelligent young man who was not obviously hysterical, anxious or dysphoric. A 'mini' mental status exam (serial sevens, three objects, writing, orientation in time and place, etc.) revealed no obvious deficits in higher functions, and there was no evidence of dementia. The most striking aspects of his disorder were that he regarded his father as an 'imposter' and he had a similar, although less compelling, delusion about his mother. When asked why he thought his father was an imposter his response was 'He looks exactly like my father but he really isn't. He's a nice guy, but he isn't my father, Doctor'.

(Hirstein & Ramachandran, 1997, p. 438)

Case 3: anosognosia for hemiplegia

Patient L.A.-O (clinical record NA 472, 1980) was a 65-year-old, right-handed woman who was admitted to the emergency department of our hospital on the evening of 2 July 1980. Shortly before admission she had suddenly developed left hemiplegia without loss of consciousness. Alert and cooperative, she claimed that the reason for her hospitalization was sudden weakness and annoying paresthesia of the right limbs; her narrative, supplied in a mild state of anxiety, was indeed accompanied by sustained massage of the allegedly hyposthenic right inferior limb. She also claimed that the left hand did not belong to her but had been forgotten in the ambulance by another patient. On request, she admitted without hesitation that her left shoulder was part of her body and inferentially came to the same conclusion as regards her left arm and elbow, given, as she remarked, the evident continuity of those members. She was elusive about the forearm but insisted in denying ownership of the left hand, even when it had been passively placed on the right side of her trunk. She could not explain why her rings happened to be worn by the fingers of the alien hand.

(Bisiach & Geminiani, 1991, pp. 32–33)

This book tries to answer three questions about delusions:

(1) *The nature question*: What is a delusion? In particular, what kind of mental state is it? The standard answer in psychiatry is that delusions are beliefs. This idea, called 'the doxasticism about delusions', is the standard view in psychiatry, and it is what I presupposed when I said in the beginning of this chapter that a delusion is 'a belief that is held despite obvious counterevidence and that is not explained by the person's social, cultural, or religious background'. But is doxasticism really true? Delusions have a number of peculiar features that are not belief-like. For instance, delusions do not seem to have the belief-like sensitivity to evidence. Is the fact that delusions have these peculiar features consistent with the doxastic conception of delusions?

(2) *The pathology question*: Delusions (in the clinical sense) are pathological mental states. This means that delusions, together with other symptoms, warrant clinical diagnoses and treatments.[3] Why are delusions pathological? What distinguishes pathological delusions from non-pathological mental states, such as non-pathological irrational beliefs? Are delusions pathological because they are more irrational than non-pathological irrational beliefs? Or, are they pathological because they are stranger than non-pathological irrational beliefs?

(3) *The etiology question*: What is the cause of a delusion? How is it formed? It is widely believed that delusions (at least many of them) are formed in response to some abnormal data.[4] Perhaps a delusion is the explanatory hypothesis a person adopts to make sense of abnormal data (e.g., the Capgras delusion as an explanation of the abnormal data generated by abnormal autonomic activities). But do abnormal data explain

everything about the process of delusion formation? Are abnormal data sufficient for someone to form a delusion? If not, what are the additional factors?

In the previous debates on delusions, these questions tend to be discussed independently from each other and in relation to different lines of inquiry: the nature question has been discussed mainly in the philosophy of mind; the etiology question, in contrast, has been examined in psychiatry and cognitive science; and the pathology question has been a topic in the philosophy of psychiatry.[5] However, discussing these questions separately is potentially problematic because they are closely related; the answer to one question can have implications for how another question is answered. For example, if your answer to the nature question is that delusions are beliefs, then you might answer the etiology question by saying that delusions are the product of some troubles in the belief formation process. Again, if your answer to the etiology question is that delusions are the product of some troubles in the process of belief formation, then you might answer the pathology question by saying that delusions are pathological because of the troubles. I will say more about the connections between these questions in the following chapters.

In this book, I take the connections between the three questions very seriously. My discussions of the questions are interrelated in such a way that my answers to them constitute a unified and coherent understanding of delusions. The central hypothesis of this book, which I call 'the malfunctional belief hypothesis', is that *delusions are malfunctional beliefs*. They belong to the category of belief and, hence, doxasticism is correct (which is my answer to the nature question). However, unlike non-pathological irrational beliefs, they fail to perform some functions of belief (which is the crucial part of my answer to the pathology question). More precisely, delusions directly or indirectly involve some malfunctioning cognitive mechanisms.[6] And an empiricist account of the delusion formation process (which answers the etiology question) makes the malfunctional belief hypothesis empirically credible.

The category of heart, according to one view,[7] is defined in terms of the distinctively heart-like function, i.e., the function of pumping blood. All (and only) members of this category *have* the function of pumping blood. But this does not mean that all the members of this category actually *perform* the function of pumping blood. Diseased or malformed hearts *have* the function of pumping blood and thus belong to the category of heart, but they do not *perform* the function. In other words, they are malfunctional hearts. A delusion, according to my hypothesis, is analogous to a diseased or malformed heart. The category of belief, just like the category of heart, is defined in terms of distinctively belief-like functions, which I tentatively call 'doxastic functions'. This is the basic idea of teleo-functionalism, which is the theoretical foundation of this book. (I will say more about teleo-functionalism in the next section.) All (and the only) members of the category of belief *have* doxastic functions. But this does not mean that all the members actually *perform* the functions. Delusions, according to my hypothesis, *have* doxastic functions and thus belong to the category of belief, but they do not *perform* the functions (or, more precisely, delusions directly or indirectly involve some cognitive mechanisms that fail to perform their functions). They are malfunctional beliefs.

Here is a brief overview of this book:

> *Chapter 2: Nature.* The central puzzle concerning the nature question comes from a seemingly incoherent pair of ideas: Delusions are beliefs (the doxasticism about delusions), and delusions have a number of features that are not belief-like (the causal difference thesis). Both ideas are at least *prima facie* plausible, but there is a clear tension between them. One solution to the puzzle is to endorse one and deny the other. This 'incompatibilist' response assumes that the two ideas are not compatible with each other and hence at least one of them should be rejected. Teleo-functionalism about beliefs, on the other hand, suggests an alternative, 'compatibilist' response, according to which the two ideas do not rule out one another. For example, there is nothing incoherent with the idea that diseased or malformed hearts belong to the category of heart despite the fact that they have some features that are not heart-like, e.g., failing to pump blood. Similarly, according to teleo-functionalism, there is nothing incoherent about the idea that delusions belong to the category of belief despite the fact that they have some features that are not belief-like.
>
> *Chapter 3: Pathology.* This chapter explores the features of delusions that are responsible for their being pathological. First, I critically examine the proposals according to which delusions are pathological because of their strangeness, their extreme irrationality, their resistance to folk psychological explanations, and the impaired responsibility–grounding capacities of people with delusions. The proposals are problematic because they invite some counterexamples as well as theoretical difficulties. An alternative account comes from Wakefield's harmful dysfunction analysis of disorder, according to which a disorder is a condition that involves harmful malfunctions (or dysfunctions). Congestive heart failure, for example, is a disorder because a heart is harmfully malfunctioning in that condition. Following Wakefield, I will argue that a delusion is a disordered or pathological mental state because it is a harmfully malfunctional state.

Chapter 4: Etiology. This chapter defends 'the empiricism about delusions', according to which delusions are formed in response to abnormal data. More precisely, this chapter defends a particular kind of empiricism called 'the two-factor theory'. The two-factor theory states that abnormal data constitute a causal factor ('the first factor' or 'factor 1'), but another causal factor ('the second factor' or 'factor 2') is also needed to explain the process of delusion formation. I will provide an inference-to-the-best-explanation argument for the two-factor theory. Among other theories, the two-factor theory provides the best explanation of relevant empirical and clinical observations. I will also discuss the prediction-error theory, which is another influential theory of the process of delusion formation. I will show that the central ideas of the prediction-error theory can be incorporated in the two-factor framework to form a hybrid theory. The hybrid theory inherits the theoretical and empirical merits of the two-factor theory and the prediction-error theory and provides a unified account of many kinds of delusions, including the ones that are explained by the two-factor theory and the ones that are explained by the prediction-error theory.

1.2   Teleo-functionalism

1.2.1   Dry-functionalism and teleo-functionalism

The discussions in the book are based on a particular theory of beliefs, namely teleo-functionalism about beliefs (and propositional attitudes in general). The malfunctional belief hypothesis, which is the central hypothesis of this book, presupposes teleo-functionalism.

Some might prefer being neutral on the theory of belief when discussing delusions. Being neutral on 'big' issues, like the issue of the nature of belief, is a good strategy in many other contexts, but it is not realistic in the context of my discussions. For example, it is difficult to say something significant and meaningful about whether delusions are beliefs or not (the nature question) without being committed to a particular theory of belief.[8] Alternatively, some might prefer relying on some common commitments that are shared by all theories of belief, rather than a particular theory. But the common commitment approach is not very promising either because it presupposes the dubious assumption that all theories of belief (including dry-functionalism, teleo-functionalism, reductive physicalism, eliminative physicalism, interpretationism, phenomenalism, etc.) share some ideas that are informative enough in discussing delusions.

Defending teleo-functionalism as the overall best theory of belief is not the aim of this book. Discussing the overall best theory of belief requires a variety of considerations that go beyond the scope of this book. One might think of this book as simply presupposing teleo-functionalism because of its usefulness in understanding delusions. Or, alternatively, one might think of this book as supporting teleo-functionalism by revealing another context (i.e., the context of understanding delusions) in which the theory is explanatorily useful.

I will now describe the basic ideas of teleo-functionalism and explain why it is particularly useful for understanding delusions and, possibly, pathological mental states in general.

Borrowing the terminology from Godfrey-Smith (1998), I distinguish two basic forms of functionalism: dry-functionalism and teleo-functionalism. According to the former, mental states are individuated by the causal roles they play (or are disposed to play). According to the latter, mental states are individuated by the functions they have.

The difference between dry-functionalism and teleo-functionalism comes down to the difference between causal roles and functions. The causal roles of pain are the roles it plays in the causal interaction with inputs, outputs, and other mental states. For example, the causal roles of pain include the role of being caused by tissue damage, the role of causing groaning or writhing, etc. On the other hand, the functions of pain are its effects, consequences, or performances, for which it has been selected in evolutionary history. Arguably, one of the functions of pain is to defend tissues from physical damages; pain has been selected for defending tissues from physical damage.

The crucial difference between causal role and function is that only the latter makes sense of the idea of malfunction; it is possible for something to have the function F without actually performing F.[9] This is possible because having the function F is a historical property, namely the property of having the right kind of history. And something can have the right kind of history without actually doing F. For example, it is possible that a mental state has the function of defending tissues from physical damage without actually performing the function. This is possible because having the function of defending tissues from physical damage is having the right kind of history (i.e., the history in which the mental state was selected for defending tissues from physical damage), and a mental state can have the right kind of history without actually defending tissues from physical damage. In contrast, the idea of malfunction does not make sense when it comes to causal roles. It is not possible for something to play the causal role R without actually doing R. If it does not do R, then it does not play the causal role R. For example, it is not possible for a mental state to play the causal roles of pain without actually causing groaning or writhing. If it does not cause groaning or writhing, then it does not play the causal roles of pain.[10]

Let me be more precise about the term 'function' used in this book. As I noted above, the term 'function' is used according to the following definition:

the functions of X (or the functions X has) are the effects, consequences, or performances for which X has been selected in evolutionary history. This is an etiological (or evolutionary) definition of function, sometimes called the 'strong' etiological (or evolutionary) definition. The 'strong' definition is sometimes contrasted with the 'weak' definition, which does not require a past selection. It only requires a past contribution to fitness (Buller, 1998). Another evolutionary definition, the 'modern' definition, requires that the relevant selection happened relatively recently in evolutionary history (Godfrey-Smith, 1994). The distinctions between these evolutionary defini-tions are certainly important in the context of the philosophy of biology, but not in the context of my discussion. To keep things simple, I stick to the 'strong' definition in this book.

I use the term 'function' in an evolutionary sense. I do not assume, however, that the term is used in an etiological sense by biologists. Some philosophers of biology do think that the term is used in an etiological sense by biologists, or the concept 'function' in the field of biology is an etiological one (e.g., Neander, 1991a, 1991b). But understanding the term 'function' or the concept 'function' in the field of biology is a separate issue, and I have nothing to say about the issue in this book. I adopt an etiological definition of function, not because the term 'function' is actu-ally used in the etiological sense in biology but because it is useful; the etiological definition is useful for articulating my commitments as a teleo-functionalist. Millikan (1989a) nicely summarizes this pragmatic attitude towards the definition of function:

> The point of the notion 'proper function' [which is Millikan's etio-logical concept of 'function'] was/is mainly to gather together certain phenomena under a heading or category that can be used produc-tively in the construction of various explanatory theories. The ulti-mate defense of such a definition can only be a series of illustration of its usefulness.
>
> (p. 289)

I will now describe dry-functionalism and teleo-functionalism in more detail.

Dry-functionalism: Dry-functionalism individuates mental states in terms of their causal roles. Belief, for example, is defined in terms of distinctively belief-like causal roles. I call them 'doxastic causal roles'. Here is a simple dry-functionalist definition:

Dry-functionalism about beliefs

Beliefs are the mental states that play (or are disposed to play) doxastic causal roles.

To play doxastic causal roles is to be causally connected to inputs, outputs, and other mental states in a distinctively belief-like way. Dry-functionalists tend not to provide detailed specifications of doxastic causal roles. But it is widely assumed that playing doxastic causal roles includes being sensitive (enough) to evidential inputs, having (enough) action-guiding capacity, and being coherent (enough) with other beliefs as well as other mental states.

Dry-functionalism can come in different forms. A version of dry-functionalism that I call 'representational dry-functionalism' claims that beliefs are representational items that play doxastic causal roles, where 'representational items' are understood as discrete, causally efficacious entities with an appropriate structure (e.g., a sentence-like structure or a map-like structure).

What I call 'boxological dry-functionalism' claims that to believe something is to have a representational item in the 'belief-box' (e.g., Nichols & Stich, 2003). The 'belief-box' is typically defined in terms of doxastic causal roles. For instance, for an item to be in the 'belief box' might simply be for it to play doxastic causal roles, in which case boxological dry-functionalism is just a different expression of representational dry-functionalism.

Dispositionalism (e.g., Schwitzgebel, 2001, 2002, 2010) might be conceived of as a stripped-down version of dry-functionalism, which, unlike representational dry-functionalism or boxological dry-functionalism, does not care about what goes on inside the head of a believer. According to dispositionalism, for a person to believe something is for the person to be disposed to behave, think, and feel in a particular way, as if there is an internal representational item that plays doxastic causal roles.

There are some subtle differences between different forms of dry-functionalism, but for the sake of simplicity I will focus on the simple version of it.

Teleo-functionalism: Teleo-functionalism individuates mental states in terms of their functions. Teleo-functionalism is sometimes regarded as being immune to imaginary counterexamples put forward against dry-functionalism (e.g., Sober, 1985), such as the Chinese Nation case. In psychology, some researchers appeal to teleo-functionalist ideas when defining some mental states. Emotions, for example, are often defined by their evolutionary purposes and functions (e.g., Cosmides & Tooby, 2000; Nesse, 1990).

Here is a simple teleo-functionalist definition of beliefs: beliefs are the mental states with distinctively belief-like functions. I call them 'doxastic functions'.

Teleo-functionalism about beliefs

Beliefs are the mental states with doxastic functions.

'Doxastic function' is just a placeholder notion. The exact nature of doxastic functions is an open empirical issue.[11] I assume that teleo-functionalism works as a scientific reduction of beliefs (e.g., Braddon-Mitchell & Jackson, 1997; Papineau, 2001). Scientists discovered what lightning is (i.e., electric discharge) by empirically investigating the nature of the phenomenon that we typically refer to as 'lightening'. Analogously, we are supposed to discover what doxastic functions are by empirically investigating (in cognitive psychology, evolutionary psychology, neuroscience, etc.) the states that we typically refer to as 'beliefs'.

Just like dry-functionalism, teleo-functionalism can come in different forms. According to homuncular teleo-functionalism, for example, an agent with a mind is constituted by simple subsystems (homunculi) with some functions. And those subsystems are, in turn, constituted by even simpler subsubsystems with even simpler functions, and so on. And mental states are defined in terms of the states of those subsystems, subsubsystems, etc. (e.g., Lycan, 1987; Sterelny, 1990). Lycan, for example, proposes to 'type-identify a mental state with the property of having such-and-such an institutionally characterized state of affairs obtaining in one (or more) of one's appropriate homunctional departments of subagencies' (Lycan, 1987, p. 41).

What I call 'the aim account of belief' maintains that beliefs are distinguished from other attitudes by their distinctive aims (e.g., truth). This account can be a teleo-functionalist theory when the notion of 'aim' is explained in terms of functions. Velleman, for example, defends a view of this kind: 'If a cognitive state isn't regulated by mechanisms designed to track the truth, then it isn't a belief: it's some other kind of cognition. That's why aiming at the truth is constitutive of belief' (Velleman, 2000, p. 17).[12]

Teleosemantics (e.g., Dretske, 1986, 1997; Millikan, 1984, 1989b) could be a kind of teleo-functionalism as well. Although teleosemantics is often understood as the theory of content (e.g., the content of beliefs), it can have an implicit teleological theory of attitudes (e.g., the attitude of believing). This is particularly clear in Millikan's version of teleosemantics, in which representational content and attitudes are inseparably related to each other.[13] I will say more about teleosemantics in 1.2.2.

For the sake of simplicity, I will focus on the simple form of teleo-functionalism in this book. I suspect, however, that adopting another form of teleo-functionalism would not change my arguments and conclusions.

Here are some notes for clarification.

First, I assume that the distinction between dry-functionalism and teleo-functionalism is a reasonable one. But I do not assume that the teleo/dry distinction is exclusive. For example, there could be some hybrid positions that appeal to both causal roles and functions in individuating mental states. For the sake of simplicity, however, I only talk about pure dry-functionalism and pure teleo-functionalism in this book. I do not assume that the teleo/dry distinction is exhaustive, either. There could be other forms of functionalism.

An example is normative functionalism, which individuates mental states in terms of distinctively belief-like norms (e.g., Zangwill, 1998). For the sake of simplicity, however, I focus on the contrast between dry-functionalism and teleo-functionalism.[14]

Second, I will not say anything about the best form of functionalism or, more generally, the best theory of belief. I only make a weak assumption; dry-functionalism is not 'the only game in town', although it is more popular than other theories, including teleo-functionalism. I assume that teleo-functionalism is a live option, and it is a viable alternative to dry-functionalism. There are important objections to teleo-functionalism. For instance, teleo-functionalism seems to imply that Swampman (i.e., the imaginary physical duplicate of Donald Davidson created by a lightning bolt hitting a swamp) does not have any beliefs, which some might find counterintuitive. Again, teleo-functionalism does not get off the ground without some adaptationist assumptions about human cognition, which some might find problematic. These objections are certainly important, but I will not address them here because, first, they will take us too far away from the main discussion of this book, and second, they do not necessarily make dry-functionalism 'the only game in town'. There are several ways in which teleo-functionalists can respond to them.[15]

Setting those objections aside, there are some other objections that might be worth considering for the purpose of clarifying my commitments. I introduced teleo-functionalism with an analogy between the category of heart and the category of belief; the former is defined in terms of the function of pumping blood and the latter is defined in terms of doxastic functions. The first objection to the heart-belief analogy is that, unlike the category of heart, the category of belief is just a folk psychological category that is not grounded in 'biological reality'.

As I already pointed out, teleo-functionalism involves a form of scientific reduction of beliefs. 'Lightening' started as a folk notion in the history of the concept, but later a 'lightening' was scientifically reduced into an electric discharge. Similarly, 'belief' started as a folk notion in the history of the concept, but, according to teleo-functionalism, a 'belief' is reduced into a state with doxastic functions. In addition, even if it is granted that beliefs are not 'biologically real' in some sense, the cognitive mechanisms underlying and realizing our doxastic capacity are 'biologically real' entities. As we will see in Chapter 2, beliefs are defined in terms of the functions of these cognitive mechanisms according to my version of teleo-functionalism.

The second objection to the heart-belief analogy is that, unlike hearts, we do not have a clear idea about the functions of beliefs. Thanks to Harvey's discovery, we know that hearts have the function of pumping blood. And it makes sense to define the category of heart in terms of that function. On the other hand, we do not know so much about 'doxastic functions', and hence the idea of defining beliefs in terms of 'doxastic functions' is not very informative.

It turns out that this is not a peculiar problem for teleo-functionalism; it is a general problem for many, if not all, theories of belief. For instance, in *A Treatise of Human Nature*, Hume famously defines beliefs in terms of their distinctive phenomenal feeling (strong 'force' and 'vivacity'), but he says that it is impossible to describe or characterize the distinctive phenomenal feeling of beliefs: 'I confess, that 'tis impossible to explain perfectly this feeling or manner of conception' (Hume, 1978, p. 629). Dry-functionalism has a similar problem. It defines beliefs in terms of doxastic causal roles, but as Schwitzgebel (2015) points out, dry-functionalists typically do not say much about what doxastic causal roles exactly are and different philosophers have different conceptions of doxastic causal roles.

Another, and more important, response to the objection is that my discussions of delusions in this book do not presuppose a specific account of doxastic functions. For example, I will argue in Chapter 2 that delusions have doxastic functions, but, as we will see, this can be shown without a specific account of doxastic functions.

That said, I tentatively propose a view of doxastic functions based on Ramsey's (2000, p. 238) famous idea that a belief is 'a map of neighbouring space by which we steer'. Ramsey says that beliefs are 'maps', which suggests that beliefs, just like maps, are supposed to represent something accurately. He also says that 'we steer by' beliefs, which suggests that beliefs, just like maps, are supposed to guide our actions. According to what I call 'Ramseyanism', representing accurately and guiding actions are the doxastic functions. I propose Ramseyanism as an example, only for the purpose of illustrating how teleo-functionalism might work. Although I suspect that Ramseyanism is not far from the truth, I admit that Ramseyanism (or, more specifically, the idea of accurate-representing function) has *prima facie* difficulty in dealing with some kinds of beliefs, such as religious beliefs, moral judgments, or positive illusions (i.e., unrealistically favorable beliefs that people have about themselves and people close to them).

1.2.2   Why teleo-functionalism?

Teleo-functionalism is particularly attractive for the purpose of this book, namely making sense of delusions and possibly pathological mental states in general. The reason for this will be clarified in later chapters, but the basic idea is simple: There is a sense in which delusions, and pathological mental states in general, are 'defective', and teleo-functionalism helps us to make sense of 'defectiveness'.

Teleo-functionalism regards mental state categories, including the category of belief, as function categories (i.e., the categories that are defined in terms of functions). As Millikan points out, the distinctive feature of the function categories is that they can include defective members of the categories: 'an obvious fact about function categories is that their members can always be defective – diseased, malformed, injured, broken, dis-functional, etc., – hence unable to perform the very functions by which they get their names' (Millikan, 1989a, p. 295).

Suppose that the category of heart is a function category, defined in terms of the function of pumping blood. Something is a heart if and only if it has the function of pumping blood. However, some members of that category (e.g., diseased hearts, malformed hearts, etc.) are defective; they fail to perform the function in terms of which the category of heart is defined. These hearts *have* the function of pumping blood (and hence are the member of the category of heart) but fail to *perform* the function (and hence are defective).

According to teleo-functionalism, mental state categories, such as the category of belief, are function categories. The category of belief, for example, is defined in terms of doxastic functions. Something is a belief if and only if it has doxastic functions. But some members of the category of belief are defective; they fail to perform the functions in terms of which the category of belief is defined. These beliefs *have* doxastic functions (and hence are the members of the category of belief) but fail to *perform* the functions (and hence are defective). And my hypothesis is that delusions are the defective members of the category of belief. This idea might be applied to other kinds of pathological mental states; addictive desires are the defective members of the category of desire, pathological anxieties are the defective members of the category of anxiety, and so on.

Dry-functionalism, on the other hand, regards mental state categories as causal categories (i.e., the categories that are defined in terms of causal roles). Unlike function categories, causal categories cannot include defective members. Let us suppose that a category C is a causal category, defined in terms of a causal role R. If something plays R, then it is a member of C, in which case there is nothing defective about it. If, in contrast, it fails to play R, then it is not a member of C in the first place (rather than a defective member of C). Either way, therefore, it is not a defective member of C.

One might think, for example, that a belief is 'defective' when it fails to play doxastic causal roles. This idea does not work for an obvious reason; if a mental state fails to play doxastic causal roles, then it is simply not a belief (rather than a defective belief). My desire for beer, for example, fails to play doxastic causal roles and, thus, is not a belief (rather than a defective belief). It is in fact a non-defective member of another category, namely the category of desire. Alternatively, one might think that a belief is 'defective' when it is a borderline case, i.e., when it is not clear whether it plays doxastic causal roles or not. But, as Millikan (1989a) points out, there is a crucial difference between 'defective cases' and 'borderline cases' because 'the notion "defective" is a normative notion' (p. 296).

The notion of 'defective' is normative; to say that something is defective is to say that it deviates from the way in which it is supposed to be. The notion of 'borderline' is not normative in this sense. Defective items might not be borderline items. For example, diseased hearts are defective hearts, but they are not borderline hearts. They are clear members of the category of heart. Again, borderline items might not be defective items. For example, we might discover a new animal species with an internal organ with some heart-like features and some non-heart-like features. Perhaps we might conclude that it a borderline case, but this does not imply that the organ is defective. There is nothing defective about the organ as long as it is working well according to its own standard. I will say more about defectiveness in Chapter 4.

Teleo-functionalism makes sense of the idea of defective mental states. This insight is widely shared among teleosemanticists who are trying to explain the misrepresenting mental states, i.e., the mental states that are 'defective' in representing objects or facts. The fundamental idea of teleosemantics is that the possibility of malfunction, i.e., the possibility that something fails to perform the function it has, is the key to understanding the possibility of misrepresentation. Millikan (2004) nicely expresses the idea as follows:

> False representations are representations, yet they fail to represent. How can that be? It can be in the same way that something can be a can opener but be too dull and hence fail to open cans, or something can be a coffee maker yet fail to make coffee because the right ingredients were not put in or it was not turned on. They are 'representations' in the sense that the biological function of the cognitive systems that made them was to make them represent things. Falsehood is thus explained by the fact that purposes often go unfulfilled.
>
> (pp. 64–65)

Certainly, the notion of 'defectiveness' in my discussion is different from that in teleosemantics. In my discussion, 'defective' means 'pathological' or something related to it. In teleosemantics, in contrast, 'defective' means 'misrepresenting'. These two meanings of 'defective' are different, but they partially overlap. (For example, pathological delusions are typically false.) The differences will be discussed in Chapter 4.

Notes

1 Defining delusion is not very easy. Some definitions have been proposed, but none of them is free from problems. According to *The Diagnostic and Statistical Manual of Mental Disorders, Fifth Edition* (DSM-5), for example, a delusion is a 'false belief based on incorrect inference about external reality that is firmly held despite what almost everyone else believes and despite what constitutes incontrovertible and obvious proof or evidence to the contrary. The belief is not ordinarily accepted by other members of the person's culture or subculture (i.e., it is not an article of religious faith). When a false belief involves a value judgment, it is regarded as a delusion only when the judgment is so extreme as to defy credibility' (American Psychiatric Association, 2013, p. 819). However, this definition (or, more precisely, the definition in DSM-IV, which is not very different from this definition) is highly controversial. See, e.g., Davies, Coltheart, Langdon, and Breen (2001) and Coltheart, Langdon, and McKay (2011).

2 But I do not rule out the possibility of the polythematic Capgras delusion. This contradicts the popular assumption that monothematicity is an essential feature of the Capgras delusion (e.g., Coltheart, 2013). This assumption, however, faces a problem; we cannot rule out *a priori* the possibility that the Capgras delusion co-occurs with the delusions about other themes. In defense of the assumption, Coltheart (2013) suggests a solution; the Capgras delusion is essentially monothematic 'if, in reports of the occurrence of [the Capgras delusion], it is frequently the case that the patient has just a single delusional belief, or at most a small set of delusional beliefs concerned with a single theme' (p. 104). But this solution is vague (how frequently should it be the case?) and potentially problematic (what if it turns out that the person has the Capgras delusion typically has delusional beliefs about multiple themes?; c.f., Bell et al., 2017).

3 But delusion-like beliefs can be present in non-clinical populations (e.g., Freeman et al., 2005) and can be created by hypnosis (e.g., Connors, Barnier, Coltheart, Cox, & Langdon, 2012). But these delusion-like beliefs are not medically treated in typical cases.

4 I use the phrase 'abnormal data' rather than 'abnormal experience' because the former is more theoretically neutral than the latter (e.g., Coltheart, Menzies, & Sutton, 2010). For example, some argue that the Capgras delusion is formed in response to an abnormal conscious experience: e.g., 'people who suffer from this kind of [brain] damage are subject to an anomalous perceptual experience – an experience of seeing a face that looks just like their relative, but without experiencing the affective response that would normally be part and parcel of that experience' (Stone & Young, 1997, p. 337). In contrast, others argue that the Capgras delusion is formed in response to an abnormal unconscious input: e.g., 'the abnormality in Capgras delusion, which prompts the exercise of abductive inference in an effort to generate a hypothesis to explain this abnormality, is not an abnormality of which the patient is aware' (Coltheart et al., 2010, p. 264). In my terminology, the phrase 'abnormal data' is compatible with both hypotheses.

5 There are some exceptions. For example, Gerrans (2013, 2014), Hohwy (2013), and Hohwy and Rajan (2012) are keenly aware of the connection between the nature question and the etiology question. Gerrans (2014), however, seems to think that the focus should be on the etiology question rather than the nature question: 'The methodology I recommend is to pay close attention to and

describe the cognitive properties of the neural mechanisms that produce delusion. . . . If our project is to explain why some one says that her family has been replaced my doubles, it is not clear that the concept of belief, anchored as if it is in conceptual debates about the nature of rationality, needs to play a large role in that explanation' (p. xiv).

6 They involve malfunctioning mechanisms directly when belief-forming mechanisms are malfunctioning. They involve malfunctioning mechanisms indirectly when some other mechanisms that are causally related to belief-forming mechanisms (e.g., perceptual mechanisms) are malfunctioning. See Chapter 3 for more details.

7 'Most biological categories are only definable in functional terms. For instance, "heart" cannot be defined except by reference to the function of hearts because no description purely in terms of morphological criteria could demarcate hearts from non-hearts' (Neander, 1991a, p. 180). But also see, e.g., Amundson and Lauder (1994).

8 In discussing the nature question, for example, Bortolotti (2009) presupposes an interpretationist theory, Schwitzgebel (2012) and Tumulty (2011) presuppose a dispositionalist theory, Egan (2009) presupposes a representationalist theory, and Clutton (2018) presupposes a cognitive phenomenalist theory.

9 This is, strictly speaking, weaker than my definition of malfunction because this definition does not rule out what I call 'misfunction', which is distinguished from malfunction. See Chapter 3 for more details.

10 An objection to this is that the idea of malfunction does make sense if malfunction is defined as follows: X malfunctions if and only if X fails to play a causal role, R, that is typical (or most) members of the group to which X belongs actually play (e.g., Godfrey-Smith, 1993; Roe & Murphy, 2011). See, e.g., Neander (1995) for a response to this objection. Another objection is that it is actually not the case that function in the etiological sense makes sense of the idea of malfunction (Davies, 2000, 2001). See, e.g., Sullivan-Bissett (2017) for a response to this objection.

11 The same thing would be true about 'doxastic causal roles' according to empirical functionalism or psychofunctionalism.

12 See also Steglich-Petersen (2017) and Sullivan-Bissett and Bortolotti (2017).

13 'On the theory proposed, intentional representations always come with propositional attitudes attached. . . . There are not and could not be intentional representations that lacked attitude. There are no intentional representations without purposes, and having a purpose guarantees attitude' (Millikan, 2004, p. 81).

14 See Bayne (2011) for a normative functionalist discussion of the nature question.

15 For the responses to the Swampman objection, see, e.g., Millikan (1996) Neander (1996), and Papineau (2001). For the responses to the adaptationism objection, see, e.g., Buller (2006) and Okasha (2003).

References

American Psychiatric Association. (2013). *Diagnostic and statistical manual of mental disorders* (5th ed.). Washington, DC: American Psychiatric Association.

Amundson, R., & Lauder, G. V. (1994). Function without purpose. *Biology and Philosophy*, *9*(4), 443–469.

Bayne, T. (2011). Delusions as doxastic states: Contexts, compartments, and commitments. *Philosophy, Psychiatry, & Psychology, 17*(4), 329–336.

Bell, V., Marshall, C., Kanji, Z., Wilkinson, S., Halligan, P., & Deeley, Q. (2017). Uncovering Capgras delusion using a large-scale medical records database. *British Journal of Psychiatry Open, 3*(4), 179–185.

Bisiach, E., & Geminiani, G. (1991). Anosognosia related to hemiplegia and hemianopia. In G. P. Prigatano & D. L. Shacter (Eds.), *Awareness of deficit after brain injury* (pp. 17–39). New York, NY: Oxford University Press.

Bortolotti, L. (2009). *Delusions and other irrational beliefs*. New York, NY: Oxford University Press.

Braddon-Mitchell, D., & Jackson, F. (1997). The teleological theory of content. *Australasian Journal of Philosophy, 75*(4), 474–489.

Buller, D. J. (1998). Etiological theories of function: A geographical survey. *Biology and Philosophy, 13*(4), 505–527.

Buller, D. J. (2006). *Adapting minds: Evolutionary psychology and the persistent quest for human nature*. Cambridge, MA: The MIT Press.

Clutton, P. (2018). A new defence of doxasticism about delusions: The cognitive phenomenological defence. *Mind & Language*, online first. Retrieved from https://doi.org/10.1111/mila.12164.

Coltheart, M. (2013). On the distinction between monothematic and polythematic delusions. *Mind & Language, 28*(1), 103–112.

Coltheart, M., Langdon, R., & McKay, R. (2011). Delusional belief. *Annual Review of Psychology, 62*, 271–298.

Coltheart, M., Menzies, P., & Sutton, J. (2010). Abductive inference and delusional belief. *Cognitive Neuropsychiatry, 15*(1–3), 261–287.

Connors, M. H., Barnier, A. J., Coltheart, M., Cox, R. E., & Langdon, R. (2012). Mirrored-self misidentification in the hypnosis laboratory: Recreating the delusion from its component factors. *Cognitive Neuropsychiatry, 17*(2), 151–176.

Cosmides, L., & Tooby, J. (2000). Evolutionary psychology and the emotions. In M. Lewis & J. M. Haviland-Jones (Eds.), *Handbook of emotions* (Vol. 2, pp. 91–115). New York, NY: Guilford Press.

Davies, M., Coltheart, M., Langdon, R., & Breen, N. (2001). Monothematic delusions: Towards a two-factor account. *Philosophy, Psychiatry, & Psychology, 8*(2), 133–158.

Davies, P. S. (2000). Malfunctions. *Biology and Philosophy, 15*(1), 19–38.

Davies, P. S. (2001). *Norms of nature: Naturalism and the nature of functions*. Cambridge, MA: The MIT Press.

Dawkins, R. (2006). *The god delusion*. London: Bantam Press.

Dretske, F. I. (1986). Misrepresentation. In R. Bogdan (Ed.), *Belief: Form, content and function* (pp. 17–36). Oxford: Clarendon Press.

Dretske, F. I. (1997). *Naturalizing the mind*. Cambridge, MA: The MIT Press.

Egan, A. (2009). Imagination, delusion, and self-deception. In T. Bayne & J. Fernández (Eds.), *Delusions and self-deception: Motivational and affective influences on belief formation* (pp. 263–280). Hove: Psychology Press.

Freeman, D., Garety, P. A., Bebbington, P. E., Smith, B., Rollinson, R., Fowler, D., . . . & Dunn, G. (2005). Psychological investigation of the structure of paranoia in a non-clinical population. *The British Journal of Psychiatry, 186*(5), 427–435.

Gerrans, P. (2013). Delusional attitudes and default thinking. *Mind & Language, 28*(1), 83–102.

Gerrans, P. (2014). *The measure of madness: Philosophy of mind, cognitive neuroscience, and delusional thought.* Cambridge, MA: The MIT Press.

Godfrey-Smith, P. (1993). Functions: Consensus without unity. *Pacific Philosophical Quarterly, 74*(3), 196–208.

Godfrey-Smith, P. (1994). A modern history theory of functions. *Noûs, 28*(3), 344–362.

Godfrey-Smith, P. (1998). *Complexity and the function of mind in nature.* Cambridge: Cambridge University Press.

Hirstein, W., & Ramachandran, V. S. (1997). Capgras syndrome: A novel probe for understanding the neural representation of the identity and familiarity of persons. *Proceedings of the Royal Society of London B: Biological Sciences, 264*(1380), 437–444.

Hohwy, J. (2013). Delusions, illusions and inference under uncertainty. *Mind & Language, 28*(1), 57–71.

Hohwy, J., & Rajan, V. (2012). Delusions as forensically disturbing perceptual inferences. *Neuroethics, 5*(1), 5–11.

Hume, D. (1978). *A treatise of human nature* (ed. L. A. Selby-Bigge, 2nd ed. by P. H. Nidditch). Oxford: Oxford University Press.

Lycan, W. G. (1987). *Consciousness.* Cambridge, MA: The MIT Press.

Millikan, R. G. (1984). *Language, thought, and other biological categories: New foundations for realism.* Cambridge, MA: The MIT Press.

Millikan, R. G. (1989a). In defense of proper functions. *Philosophy of Science, 56*(2), 288.

Millikan, R. G. (1989b). Biosemantics. *Journal of Philosophy, 86,* 281–297.

Millikan, R. G. (1996). On swampkinds. *Mind & Language, 11*(1), 103–117.

Millikan, R. G. (2004). *Varieties of meaning: The 2002 Jean Nicod lectures.* Cambridge, MA: The MIT Press.

Neander, K. (1991a). Functions as selected effects: The conceptual analyst's defense. *Philosophy of Science, 58*(2), 168–184.

Neander, K. (1991b). The teleological notion of "function". *Australasian Journal of Philosophy, 69*(4), 454–468.

Neander, K. (1995). Misrepresenting & malfunctioning. *Philosophical Studies, 79*(2), 109–141.

Neander, K. (1996). Swampman meets swampcow. *Mind & Language, 11*(1), 118–129.

Nesse, R. M. (1990). Evolutionary explanations of emotions. *Human Nature, 1*(3), 261–289.

Nichols, S., & Stich, S. P. (2003). *Mindreading: An integrated account of pretence, self-awareness, and understanding other minds.* New York, NY: Oxford University Press.

Okasha, S. (2003). Fodor on cognition, modularity, and adaptationism. *Philosophy of Science, 70*(1), 68–88.

Papineau, D. (2001). The status of teleosemantics, or how to stop worrying about swampman. *Australasian Journal of Philosophy, 79*(2), 279–289.

Ramsey, F. P. (2000). *The foundations of mathematics and other logical essays.* London: Routledge.

Roe, K., & Murphy, D. (2011). Function, dysfunction, and adaptation? In P. R. Adriaens & A. De Block (Eds.), *Maladapting minds: Philosophy, psychiatry, and evolutionary theory* (pp. 216–237). New York, NY: Oxford University Press.

Schwitzgebel, E. (2001). In-between believing. *The Philosophical Quarterly, 51*(202), 76–82.

Schwitzgebel, E. (2002). A phenomenal, dispositional account of belief. *Noûs, 36*(2), 249–275.

Schwitzgebel, E. (2010). Acting contrary to our professed beliefs or the gulf between occurrent judgment and dispositional belief. *Pacific Philosophical Quarterly, 91*(4), 531–553.

Schwitzgebel, E. (2012). Mad belief? *Neuroethics, 5*(1), 13–17.

Schwitzgebel, E. (2015). Belief. In E. N. Zalta (Ed.), *The Stanford Encyclopedia of Philosophy* (Summer 2015 ed.). Retrieved from https://plato.stanford.edu/archives/sum2015/entries/belief/.

Sober, E. (1985). Panglossian functionalism and the philosophy of mind. *Synthese, 64*(2), 165–193.

Steglich-Petersen, A. (2017). Fictional persuasion and the nature of belief. In E. Sullivan-Bissett, H. Bradley, & P. Noordhof (Eds.), *Art and belief* (pp. 174–193). New York, NY: Oxford University Press.

Sterelny, K. (1990). *The representational theory of mind: An introduction.* Oxford: Basil Blackwell.

Stone, T., & Young, A. W. (1997). Delusions and brain injury: The philosophy and psychology of belief. *Mind & Language, 12*(3–4), 327–364.

Sullivan-Bissett, E. (2017). Malfunction defended. *Synthese, 194*(7), 2501–2522.

Sullivan-Bissett, E., & Bortolotti, L. (2017). Fictional persuasion, transparency, and the aim of belief. In E. Sullivan-Bissett, H. Bradley, & P. Noordhof (Eds.), *Art and belief* (pp. 153–173). New York, NY: Oxford University Press.

Tumulty, M. (2011). Delusions and dispositionalism about belief. *Mind & Language, 26*(5), 596–628.

Velleman, D. (2000). *The possibility of practical reason.* New York, NY: Oxford University Press.

Zangwill, N. (1998). Direction of fit and normative functionalism. *Philosophical Studies, 91*(2), 173–203.

2 Nature

2.1 Overview

This chapter discusses a puzzle about the nature question. The puzzle involves a seemingly incoherent pair of ideas, both of which are at least *prima facie* plausible. One of them is what I call 'the doxasticism about delusions' (DD), according to which delusions are beliefs. The other is what I call 'the causal difference thesis' (CDT), according to which many delusions do not play doxastic causal roles. The puzzle arises from the observation that, on the one hand, both DD and CDT are plausible at least to some extent but, on the other hand, there is a clear tension between them (**2.2**).

One might think that DD and CDT are incompatible with each other and, hence, at least one of them should be rejected. This 'incompatibilism' is dominant in the recent literature on delusions. The incompatibilism tends to be associated with dry-functionalism, according to which beliefs are the mental states that play (or are disposed to play) doxastic causal roles. There are two types of incompatibilists. First, there are 'anti-DD incompatibilists' who reject DD and accept CDT (e.g., Currie, 2000; Currie & Jureidini, 2001; Currie & Ravenscroft, 2002; Dub, 2017; Frankish, 2009; Egan, 2009; Schwitzgebel, 2012; Tumulty, 2011, 2012). Anti-DD incompatibilists argue that many delusions are not beliefs because they fail to play doxastic causal roles. Second, there are 'pro-DD incompatibilists' who reject CDT and accept DD. Pro-DD incompatibilists defend the idea that delusions are beliefs by rejecting, or at least downplaying, the claim that delusions fail to play doxastic causal roles (e.g., Bayne & Pacherie, 2005; Bortolotti, 2009, 2011, 2012; Bortolotti & Broome, 2012; Reimer, 2010a, 2010b).

Both anti-DD incompatibilism and pro-DD incompatibilism are important options, but there are some worries about them (**2.3**). In this chapter, I will explore the alternative 'compatibilist' option, according to which DD and CDT could both be true at the same time. Unlike dry-functionalism, teleo-functionalism makes room for compatibilism because, according to this view, a mental state is a belief when it has doxastic functions, and a state can have doxastic functions without playing doxastic causal roles or being disposed to do so. This means that DD and CDT are at least logically compatible with each other. I will also suggest that DD and CDT are not only logically compatible with each other but also that they (DD in particular) may well be true in light of the available empirical evidence (**2.4**).

2.2 A tension

2.2.1 *Doxasticism about delusions*

I will now set up the puzzle by clarifying what DD and CDT are committed to and describing some *prima facie* reasons for holding them. I will start with DD.

According to DD, delusions are beliefs; DS in Case 2, for example, believes that his father has been replaced by an imposter. It is not the case that DS merely imagines or supposes that his father has been replaced by an imposter. The strong form of DD is a universal claim; all delusions are beliefs. The strong DD is consistent with the fact that DD is very often part of the definition of delusion in psychiatry, for instance the one in DSM-5 (see the endnote 1 in Chapter 1). There are weaker versions of DD as well; some delusions are beliefs, or typical delusions are beliefs.[1]

There are several different ways to interpret the claim that delusions are beliefs, depending on the interpretation of what the view is about. What I call 'the concept DD' is a claim about the concept 'belief'. According to the concept DD, the concept 'belief' is applicable to, for instance, DS when he sincerely claims that his father has been replaced by an imposter. What I call 'the attribution DD' is a claim about the third-personal attribution of belief for predicting and explaining observable behavior. According to the attribution DD, beliefs are third-personally attributed to people with delusions for predicting and explaining their observable behavior. For instance, the belief that his father has been replaced by an impostor is third-personally attributed to DS for predicting and explaining his observable behavior. What I call 'the mental state DD' is a claim about the mental state of believing. According to the mental state DD, DS is in the mental state of believing when he sincerely claims that his father has been replaced by an imposter.

My primary focus is on the mental state DD. In other words, I am primarily interested in the idea that people with delusions are in the mental state of believing. This is consistent with my understanding that teleofunctionalism, which is the theoretical basis of my discussions in this book, is best understood as a theory of the mental state of believing rather than the concept 'belief' or the third-personal belief attribution. It is not very likely that functions, which are determined by evolutionary history, are relevant in the application of the concept 'belief' or the practice of third-personal belief attribution. We usually do not care about evolutionary history when applying the concept 'belief' or attributing beliefs third-personally. However, it is at least a possible view that functions are relevant in individuating the mental state category of belief for the same reason that it is at least a possible (and, perhaps, plausible) view that functions are relevant in individuating the category of heart. Hereafter, the term 'DD' refers to 'the mental state DD'.[2]

DD has at least some degree of plausibility because it nicely explains a number of features of delusions. First, people with delusions sincerely assert the content of their delusions. DS, for example, sincerely asserts that his father has been replaced by an imposter (although he might hide this commitment when in conversation with people he does not trust). Second, people with delusions tend to regard their own delusions as beliefs. DS probably believes that he believes that his father has been replaced by an imposter (although he might hide this in some contexts).[3] Third, delusions are regarded as beliefs by psychiatrists who have the expert knowledge of delusions as well as the direct acquaintance with people with delusions. In fact, delusions are often described as beliefs in textbooks, diagnostic manuals, and research papers in psychiatry. Fourth, delusions are clinically distinguished from other pathological phenomena, such as hallucinations, jargon aphasia, or obsessive thoughts, and these distinctions do not seem to be arbitrary.

DD nicely explains the first feature (because typically a person who believes that P sincerely asserts that P), the second feature (because typically a person who believes that P believes that she believes that P), and the third feature (because typically a person who believes that P is judged as believing that P by those who know her psychological condition very well).

DD also helps us to make sense of the fourth feature, i.e., the clinical distinction between delusions and other pathological mental phenomena. For example, delusion as a doxastic state is distinguished from hallucination as a perceptual state.[4] Again, delusion as a doxastic abnormality is distinguished from linguistic abnormalities such as jargon aphasia. People with jargon aphasia make strange utterances due to linguistic impairments (e.g., 'Someone went into his room through the window' due to the confusion between 'window' and 'door'). In contrast, L.A.-O in Case 3 makes strange claims (e.g., 'This is not my hand, but someone else's!') not because of linguistic impairments but because of her abnormal doxastic commitments.[5] Perhaps the distinction between delusion and obsessive thought too is (at least partially) explained in terms of doxastic commitments. For instance, people with obsessive thoughts about contamination by germs tend to have a greater awareness of the strangeness of their thoughts than people with delusions, which might suggest that people in the former group do not actually believe the idea, at least not in the same serious way that people in the latter group do.

It is not my claim, however, that only DD explains the features of delusions described above. My claim is much weaker; DD provides an explanation of the features, which makes DD a *prima facie* plausible view.

2.2.2 Causal difference thesis

Let us now turn to CDT. CDT says that delusions do not causally behave in belief-like ways. Detailed specifications of doxastic causal roles are not available, but it is widely assumed that doxastic causal roles include some degree of sensitivity to evidential inputs, guidance of non-verbal actions, and coherence with other beliefs as well as other mental states. CDT is supported by numerous clinical and empirical observations that many delusions do not play these roles.

Insensitivity to evidential inputs: Delusions typically lack belief-like sensitivity to evidential inputs. In particular, delusions are notoriously insensitive to counterevidence, and this insensitivity is often regarded as one of the defining features of delusions. The definition of delusion in DSM-5 characterizes delusions as being 'firmly sustained despite what almost everyone else believes and despite what constitutes incontrovertible and obvious evidence to the contrary' (American Psychiatric Association, 2013, p. 819). In a case reported by Davies, Coltheart, Langdon, and Breen (2001), for example, a 33-year-old male with chronic schizophrenia claimed that he did not have any internal organs. He maintained his delusion about his internal organs (or lack thereof) despite the overwhelming counterevidence (e.g., testimony, physiological facts, etc.) and despite acknowledging the counterevidence.

Lack of action-guiding: Delusions sometimes fail to guide non-verbal actions. A classic observation of this phenomenon is given by Bleuler (1924):

> Other patients imagine themselves transformed into animals and even into things, and yet they usually do not adhere to one idea. Just as a patient can be the Pope, the Emperor, the Sultan, and eventually God in one person, he can also be a pig and a horse. Nevertheless, the patients rarely follow up the logic to act accordingly, as, for instance, to bark like a dog when they profess to be a dog. Although they refuse to admit the truth, they behave as if the expression is only to be taken symbolically, in the same way perhaps as when a man is insultingly called a pig.
> (p. 140)

When, for instance, a man believes that his wife has been replaced by an imposter, we expect him to act in accordance with the belief. For example, we expect that he refuses to live with the alleged imposter, calls the police, looks for his missing wife, and so on. However, these expected non-verbal actions are absent in many cases of the Capgras delusion:[6]

> Although in some cases of Capgras delusion patients act in ways that seem appropriate to their beliefs, in many other cases one finds a curious asynchrony between the firmly stated delusional belief and actions one might reasonably expect to have followed from it. . . . This failure to maintain a close co-ordination of beliefs and actions may be typical of the delusions that can follow brain injury.
>
> (Stone & Young, 1997, p. 334)

Incoherence with other mental states: Delusions are often incoherent with other beliefs. In a case reported by McKay and Cipolotti (2007), a person with the Cotard delusion, LU, claims that she is dead while being fully aware that she can move and speak and that dead people cannot move and speak. The incoherence with other beliefs is typical among 'circumscribed delusions', i.e., delusions that do not have a global impact on other beliefs the person has (e.g., Davies et al., 2001).[7] What is peculiar about circumscribed delusions is that, even though delusions are not very coherent with other things the person believes, delusions and other beliefs can cohabit without competing with each other; the person does not try to recover the coherence in the belief system by revising delusions (e.g., 'I am dead') or other beliefs (e.g., 'dead people cannot move and speak').

In addition, delusions often fail to have belief-like impact on affective states. For instance, Bovet and Parnas (1993) report the following case:

> One of our patients, a 50-year-old female with paranoid schizophrenia and delusional ideas, which she in no way enacted, lived peacefully with her mother in a small Swiss town which she had apparently never left, helping with house- and garden-keeping. She expressed her paranoid ideas about her sister, which she maintained for years quietly and without anger.
>
> (p. 588)

More impressive examples are found in cases of the Capgras delusion. A man who believes that his wife has been replaced by an imposter should exhibit negative affective responses, such as worry, anxiety, or fear unless there are some inhibiting factors. And he should find it very difficult to live happily with the alleged imposter. But sometimes people with the Capgras delusion do not exhibit negative affective responses. And even when they do, their negative affective responses tend to be reduced or limited. Some of them are friendly enough to the alleged imposters, and sometimes they even express strong positive affective feelings towards them. Lucchelli and Spinnler (2007) report a case in which a person with the Capgras delusion believed that his wife Wilma had been replaced by an imposter:[8]

> [The person] never became angry or aggressive. Even in the presence of the 'false' Wilma, his behavior did not differ in any significant way from his usual (for instance, he did not show any difference or hesitancy to share his everyday life with her). However, he was adamant that she could not possibly be his wife, although he was never able to explain his conviction.
>
> (p. 189)

Assuming that doxastic causal roles include some degree of sensitivity to evidential inputs, guidance of non-verbal actions, and coherence with other beliefs as well as other mental states, the clinical and empirical observations above seem to show that CDT is true of many delusions, i.e., many delusions do not play doxastic causal roles. Note that delusion is a very heterogeneous category (c.f., Radden, 2011). Those features above are present in some delusions but not in others. (Insensitivity to evidence is, however, very likely to be a universal feature of delusions.) Let us call these features 'delusional features' and delusions with delusional features 'problematic delusions'. The problematic-ness of a delusion is a matter of degree. The degree of problematic-ness of a delusion depends on the number of delusional features it has, as well as the degree to which it exhibits its delusional features. A delusion with two delusional features (e.g., the insensitivity to evidence and the lack of action-guidance) is, other things being equal, more problematic than the delusion with one delusional feature (e.g., the insensitivity to evidence). A delusion with a high degree of delusional features (e.g., the complete insensitivity to evidence) is, other things being equal, more problematic than the delusion with a low degree of it (e.g., the moderate insensitivity to evidence). Above I characterized CDT as the claim that many delusions fail to play doxastic causal roles. Now we can make the claim more precise; CDT says that significantly problematic delusions (i.e., delusions with a significant degree of problematic-ness) fail to play doxastic causal roles.

2.3 Incompatibilism

2.3.1 Pro-DD incompatibilism

Our puzzle is that, on the one hand, both DD and CDT are plausible at least to some extent, but, on the other hand, there is a clear tension between them. If CDT is true and significantly problematic delusions fail to play doxastic causal roles, how can it be the case that these delusions are beliefs? (I only talk about significantly problematic delusions in 2.3, although I will not repeat the phrase 'significantly problematic'.)

Pro-DD incompatibilists resolve the tension between DD and CDT by rejecting CDT. In doing so, pro-DD incompatibilists need to justify their denial of CDT despite the clinical and empirical observations in favor of it. Here, I will discuss Bortolotti's (2009, 2012) attempt, which I take to be the most sophisticated attempt to defend the pro-DD incompatibilist option.[9]

However, it should be noted that, strictly speaking, Bortolotti does not aim to refute CDT. Her aim is not to refute the claim that delusions fail to play doxastic causal roles, but to refute a slightly different claim that delusions are significantly more irrational – with respect to evidence ('epistemic irrationality'), other mental states ('procedural irrationality'), and actions ('agential rationality') – than non-delusional irrational beliefs. But Bortolotti's argument is relevant in our context because of the obvious similarity between CDT, which says that delusions fail to play doxastic causal roles, and the claim that delusions are significantly more irrational than non-delusional irrational beliefs. Indeed, both claims are supported by the same body of clinical and empirical observations. In any case, what I will discuss below is, strictly speaking, a Bortolotti-style argument against CDT.

Bortolotti's strategy is to give some concrete examples, from empirical studies and everyday observations, suggesting that delusional features are, to some extent, also present in some non-delusional irrational beliefs. She admits that delusions and non-delusional irrational beliefs are not completely equivalent; the former group is more problematic than the latter. For example, delusions are less sensitive to evidential inputs than non-delusional irrational beliefs. But this is a difference in degree, not in kind.[10] She summarizes her claims in the following:

> The delusion that I am dead is very different from the belief that the supermarket will be closed on Sunday, but this does not show that there is a categorical difference between delusions and beliefs. Here is a challenge. For each delusion, I'll give you a belief that matches the type if not the degree of irrationality of the delusion.
>
> (Bortolotti, 2009, p. 259)

> The psychological literature invites us, instead, to consider that beliefs are often badly integrated with other beliefs, unsupported by evidence, resistant to change, and behaviourally inefficacious. Once we accept that everyday beliefs can be irrational in these ways, it is a short step to

maintain that there is a continuity between everyday beliefs and clinical delusions.

(Bortolotti, 2012, p. 39)

Bortolotti provides us with many examples to support her claim that delusions and non-delusional irrational beliefs are different only in degree, not in kind. Here are some examples. Many non-delusional irrational beliefs, such as racist beliefs and religious beliefs, are insensitive to counterevidence. Typically, giving counterevidence is not very effective in challenging the racist belief that black people are lazy and intellectually incompetent, or the religious belief that God created humans separately from other animal species. Some non-delusional irrational beliefs are not coherent with other beliefs. For example, many people maintain superstitious beliefs about magic or supernatural phenomena despite their commitment to the scientific worldview (and despite their recognition that their superstitious beliefs are implausible according to the scientific worldview). Again, some non-delusional irrational beliefs do not guide non-verbal actions. For instance, people might verbally express their belief that using condoms is important because unprotected sex is dangerous, but they might not actually use condoms.

Bortolotti's argument seems to be powerful, but it can be resisted. There are two kinds of questions that are relevant in evaluating her argument:

(A) Did Bortolotti really give us examples of non-delusional beliefs with delusional features? Do the examples really exhibit delusional features? (For instance, some might think that religious beliefs are sensitive to evidence of some relevant kind, such as testimonial evidence.) Are they really beliefs? (For instance, some might deny that in the condom example people really believe that using condoms is important.)

(B) Assuming that they are genuine examples of beliefs with some delusional features, do they really undermine CDT? (For instance, someone might grant that delusional features are present in some non-delusional irrational beliefs but still insist that delusions and non-delusional irrational beliefs are importantly different.)

In the following, I will leave (A) open and will instead focus on (B). For the sake of argument, I simply grant that delusional features are also present in some non-delusional irrational beliefs; I ask only if this is enough to undermine CDT. I will not discuss (A) because, first, Bortolotti gives many examples and I am not able to examine them individually and, second, (A) does not really matter when the answer to (B) (as we will see) turns out to be 'No'.

I will now provide four reasons to think that the answer to (B) is 'No' in fact.

(1) *Degree matters*: Bortolotti takes her examples to show that the difference between delusions and non-delusional irrational beliefs is a difference in degree, not in kind. Does this really undermine CDT? Perhaps differences in degree matter. The difference in degree between X and Y could be significant enough to establish an important distinction between them. Indeed, in the standard folk psychological classification of mental states, there are some pairs of mental state categories such that the one category differs from the other in degree, not in kind. This means that a causal difference in degree is sometimes significant enough to draw a distinction between two mental state categories in the folk psychological classification.

For instance, philosophers sometimes draw a distinction between believing and accepting, but perhaps the difference between them is one of degree, not of kind. About the distinction between them, Schwitzgebel (2015) writes:

> Generally speaking, acceptance is held to be more under voluntary control of the subject than belief and more directly tied to a particular practical action in a context. For example, a scientist, faced with evidence supporting a theory, evidence acknowledged not to be completely decisive, may choose to accept the theory or not to accept it. If the theory is accepted, the scientist ceases inquiring into its truth and becomes willing to ground her own research and interpretations in that theory; the contrary if the theory is not accepted.
>
> ('2.5 Belief and Acceptance', para. 1)

Schwitzgebel's phrase 'acceptance is held to be *more* under voluntary control of the subject than belief and *more* directly tied to a particular practical action in a context' (emphasis added) suggests that even though voluntary control and connection to practical actions are more evident in acceptances, beliefs do exhibit these features to some degree. For example, it is widely acknowledged that beliefs can be influenced by voluntary control, at least indirectly. For instance, we can change our beliefs by voluntarily manipulating evidence-gathering behavior, changing the focus of attention, changing epistemic habits, and so on. Again, it is not the case that acceptance is purely practical and totally insensitive to evidence or truth. The scientist in Schwitzgebel's example might accept the theory for practical purposes. But it is important to note that she has at least some evidence for the theory. It is hard for her to accept the theory, no matter how practically useful the theory is, if she has no evidence for it whatsoever, and even harder if she has strong counterevidence against it. This shows that even acceptances are sensitive to evidence or truth to some degree.[11]

(2) *Jointly significant difference*: Bortolotti discusses delusional features ('irrationalities' in her terminology) one by one and argues that none of them create a significant dissimilarity (i.e., a dissimilarity that is significant enough to exclude delusions from the category of belief) between delusions and non-delusional irrational beliefs. She takes this to show that there is no significant dissimilarity between delusions and non-delusional irrational beliefs. However, this line of thought is problematic because it neglects the possibility that the delusional features make a significant dissimilarity jointly, even if none of them make a significant dissimilarity individually.

Here is a useful analogy. Presumably, having a high temperature itself might not be a very strong indication of illness; one can have a high temperature without being ill, for example immediately after physical exercise. Heavy sneezing itself might not be a very strong indication of illness, either; one can sneeze heavily without being ill, for example due to allergic rhinitis. Again, having a sore throat itself might not be a strong indication of illness; one can have a sore throat without being ill, for example after singing for several hours in a karaoke bar. Nonetheless, these symptoms jointly provide a strong indication of illness. If I have a high temperature, heavy sneezing, and a sore throat at the same time, then it is very likely that I am ill. Similarly, the mere fact that delusions are insensitive to counterevidence might not support CDT; some non-delusional irrational beliefs, such as racist beliefs, are insensitive to counterevidence, too. The mere fact that delusions are incoherent with other beliefs might not support CDT, either; some non-delusional irrational beliefs, such as superstitious beliefs, are incoherent with other beliefs, too. Again, the mere fact that delusions do not guide non-verbal actions might not support CDT; some non-delusional irrational beliefs, such as the belief that using condoms is important, do not guide non-verbal actions, either. Nonetheless, these delusional features jointly support CDT. If a mental state is insensitive to counterevidence, and it is incoherent with other beliefs, and it does not guide non-verbal actions, then it is very likely that the mental state does not play doxastic causal roles.

This worry is serious because multiple delusional features are often present simultaneously. In other words, it is often the case that a delusion exhibits several delusional features at the same time. Indeed, Bortolotti admits that delusions are typically 'irrational across more dimensions than non-delusional beliefs' (Bortolotti, 2012, p. 39), which means, in my terminology, that delusions typically have more delusional features than non-delusional irrational beliefs.[12]

(3) *Same argument for anti-doxastic views*: Suppose that Bortolotti is right; delusions and non-delusional irrational beliefs are different only in degree, not in kind. But this is not enough to establish that delusions do play doxastic causal roles if it turns out that delusions and other non-doxastic

mental states are different only in degree, too. For example, it might turn out that delusions and imaginings are different only in degree, in which case we cannot conclude that the causal roles of delusions are genuinely doxastic, rather than imaginative. Currie and Jones (2006) seem to accept a view of this kind:

> It may be that cognitive states do not sort themselves neatly into categorically distinct classes we should label 'beliefs' and 'imaginings', but that these categories represent vague clusterings in a space that encompasses a continuum of states for some of which we have no commonly accepted labels.
>
> (p. 312)

Currie and Jones argue that beliefs and imaginings are on a continuum and delusions are located somewhere between them. They might happily agree with Bortolotti's claim that delusions and non-delusional irrational beliefs are different only in degree, but add that the same thing is true about delusions and imaginings and that in the continuum delusions are not closer to non-delusional irrational beliefs than to imaginings.

(4) *What makes delusions pathological?*: Bortolotti's argument leaves a puzzle concerning the pathology question. She emphasizes the similarity between delusions and non-delusional irrational beliefs. But, if they are so similar, why is it that delusions are pathological while non-delusional irrational beliefs are not? Certainly, racist beliefs are not very sensitive to evidential inputs, but we typically do not think that they are pathological mental states.

It is not Bortolotti's view that there is no difference at all between delusions and non-delusional irrational beliefs. There are differences, i.e., the differences in degree. So, she might argue that the differences in degree are responsible for the fact that delusions are pathological. But this might not be a stable position. On the one hand, she needs to say that the differences in degree are not enough to make delusions non-doxastic but, on the other hand, that the differences in degree are enough to make them pathological. But can this asymmetry (where the differences in degree are significant enough in the context of pathology but not in the context of doxasticism) be really justified?

Bortolotti (2009) is aware of this issue and she tentatively suggests that delusions are pathological because they have significant negative impact on well-being:

> One possibility is that delusions are pathological in that they negatively affect the well-being and the health of the subjects who report them

(as many have already argued). Irrational beliefs that are not delusions seem less distressing, and don't seem to exhaust the cognitive resources of the subjects in the same way delusions do.

(p. 260)

Certainly, delusions negatively influence the well-being of people with delusions in many ways. They cause psychological distress, prevent them from being fully involved in social life and personal relationships, make it difficult for them to develop and exercise their abilities and talents, increase the risk of suicide, and so on. And it is very likely that there is an important link between having a negative impact on well-being and being pathological. However, having a negative impact on well-being might not be sufficient for being pathological, even if it is necessary.[13] I will say more about pathology and well-being in Chapter 3.

2.3.2   Anti-DD incompatibilism

Anti-DD incompatibilists resolve the tension between DD and CDT by rejecting DD. In other words, they deny that delusions are beliefs. What are delusions, then, if they are not beliefs? There are two available options. First, they might belong to an existing non-doxastic category, such as the category of imagination. Second, they might belong a new category, a 'bedfellow' category, according to the terminology of Bayne and Hattiangadi (2013). Here are some proposals in the literature; the first proposal exemplifies the first option, and the second and the third proposals exemplify the second option.[14]

Imagination: Currie and colleagues (Currie, 2000; Currie & Jureidini, 2001; Currie & Ravenscroft, 2002) argue that delusions are not beliefs but imaginings.[15] But, unlike other normal imaginings, delusional imaginings are peculiar in that they are misidentified as beliefs due to a metacognitive failure. For example, DS imagines, not believes, that his father has been replaced by an imposter and, at the same time, falsely believes that he believes that his father has been replaced by an imposter. This metacognitive failure is hypothesized as being caused by the failure to recognize the self-generatedness of the imagining.[16]

Bimagination: Egan (2009) proposes that delusions are not beliefs but 'bimaginings', the intermediate mental states with some belief-like features and some imagining-like features: 'Delusional subjects are in states that play a role in their cognitive economies that is in some respects like of a standard-issue, stereotypical belief that P, and in other respects like that of a standard-issue stereotypical imagining that P' (p. 268). For example, DS is bimagining, rather than believing or imagining, that his father has been replaced by an imposter.[17]

In-between beliefs: Schwitzgebel (2012) suggests that delusions are 'in-between beliefs', i.e., the intermediate states between believing and failing to believe: 'Cases of delusions are, at least sometimes (when the functional role or dispositional profile is weird enough), cases in an in-betweenish gray zone – not quite belief and not quite failure to believe' (p. 15). So, for example, DS in-between believes that his father has been replaced by an imposter, i.e., he is in the intermediate state between believing that his father has been replaced by an imposter and failing to believe it.

I do not have a knockdown argument against anti-DD incompatibilism, but I have some worries about the position. Here I set aside the issues about specific anti-DD incompatibilist proposals, such as the imagination account or the bimagination account.[18] Rather, I focus on the issues concerning anti-DD incompatibilism in general. As I noted in Chapter 1, there is a tendency among philosophers (and anti-DD incompatibilists in particular) to discuss the nature question independently from the pathology question and the etiology question. But this tendency is problematic because the three questions are interrelated. The nature question has to be discussed in relation to the pathology question and the etiology question. And my worry is that anti-DD incompatibilism might not be an attractive position when seeing the implications this position has on the pathology question and the etiology question.

Etiology: When it comes to the etiology question, the researchers who are working on the delusion formation process seem to agree on the view that delusions have a doxastic etiology; either they are produced in the same process in which non-delusional beliefs are formed, for example in response to some perceptual data, or they are produced due to some biases or impairments in the process of belief formation. The former view is often attributed to Maher (1974), who argues that the etiology of delusion is indistinguishable from the one of normal beliefs: 'The explanations (i.e. the delusions) of the patient are derived by cognitive activity that is essentially indistinguishable from that employed by non-patients, by scientists, and by people generally' (p. 103). This view might not be coherent with anti-DD incompatibilism; there is something implausible in the idea that a non-doxastic state, an imagining for example, is produced in the same process in which non-delusional beliefs are produced. The latter view is more popular in the current literature, in particular among the two-factor theorists (e.g., Coltheart, 2007; Coltheart, Langdon, & McKay, 2011; Davies et al., 2001; Langdon & Coltheart, 2000). This view does not seem to be any better in cohering with anti-DD incompatibilism than the former view; there is something implausible in the idea that a non-doxastic state, an imagining for example, is produced in the biased or impaired belief formation processes.

Currie and colleagues might not be convinced. For example, Currie and Jureidini (2001) admit that just like many other beliefs, delusions are produced in response to perceptual data, but they insist that this is perfectly compatible with (and even supportive of) their proposal because imaginings are very often triggered in response to perceptual data:

> It is characteristic of imagining to be much more easily triggered by perception than is belief. We might readily imagine that a stranger's gaunt appearance signals that he has AIDS but be rightly very resistant to believing it without further evidence. Indeed, if imagination were not easily triggered by mere appearances, pictures, plays, and movies would have very little appeal for us.
>
> (pp. 159–160)

However, the way in which delusions are triggered by perceptual data might not be similar to the way in which imaginings are triggered by perceptual data. A difference is evident when we consider relevant counterfactual facts. In their example, a person imagines that a stranger has AIDS. This imagining is counterfactually 'open' in the sense that, with the perceptual data fixed, he could have easily imagined another possibility, for example the possibility that the stranger's gaunt appearance signals that he is in an early stage of the process of turning into a zombie. Delusions, on the other hand, are counterfactually 'closed' in the sense that, for example, it is not the case that DS, with the perceptual data fixed, could have easily adopted another hypothesis, for example the hypothesis that the man in front of him is his father. I will come back to this issue later in this chapter.

Pathology: Anti-DD incompatibilists tend to emphasize the dissimilarity or the discontinuity between delusions and non-delusional beliefs. But this raises a question: If they are so different from non-delusional beliefs that they are excluded from the category of belief, why are delusions pathological?

A tempting thought is that it is partly because we think that DS actually believes that his father has been replaced by an imposter that DS is in a pathological mental state. The delusional idea is too abnormal to be seriously believed by a non-clinical person. If he does not believe it but rather imagines it, it is far from clear that he is in a pathological mental state. The delusional idea is not too abnormal to be imagined by a non-clinical person. After all, anyone with normal imaginative capacity can easily imagine that one's father has been replaced by an imposter. Similarly, delusions exhibit a number of abnormal features that might contribute to their pathological nature, but these features are only abnormal against the background assumption that they are beliefs. For instance, delusions are regarded as being abnormally insensitive to evidence (counterevidence in particular), but the insensitivity to evidence is abnormal only against the background assumption that delusions are beliefs and thus, just like other beliefs, are supposed to be sensitive to evidence. Without this assumption, there is no reason to expect delusions to be sensitive to evidence in the first place. For instance, if DS imagines (rather than believes) that his father has been replaced by an imposter, then there is no reason to expect DS to be sensitive to evidence in the first place; this means that there is no reason to regard his insensitivity to evidence to be abnormal.

Currie and colleagues might argue that the pathology of delusions is due to a metacognitive impairment because of which people mistakenly take their delusional imaginings to be beliefs. This proposal is certainly a coherent one, but it is in need of empirical justification. Empirical studies suggest metacognitive impairments in schizophrenia and, interestingly, some of them suggest an impaired capacity to distinguish mental imageries from perceptions (e.g., Anselmetti et al., 2007; Brébion et al., 2000; Jenkinson, Edelstyn, Drakeford, & Ellis, 2009). However, what these studies suggest is a misidentification at the perceptual level (i.e., a perception/mental imagery misidentification), while what Currie and colleagues expect is a misidentification at the attitudinal level (i.e., a belief/propositional imagination misidentification). The empirical evidence for the former misidentification is not the empirical evidence for the latter misidentification.

One might think that the problems outlined above do not undermine the second option for anti-DD incompatibilists, according to which delusions belong to a new category such as the category of bimagination. Certainly, the idea that an imagining can have a doxastic etiology does not sound very plausible. But the same thing might not be true about bimaginings. Perhaps bimaginings can have a doxastic etiology. After all, bimaginings are supposed to have some belief-like features, and a doxastic etiology might be one of them. However, the second option for anti-DD incompatibilists does not seem to provide a better answer to the pathology question than the first option. DS's psychological condition is pathological partly because he seriously believes, rather than merely imagines, that his father has been replaced by an imposter. The content of the delusion is too abnormal to be seriously believed by a non-clinical person. But if he does not believe it but rather bimagines it, then it is far from clear that he is in a pathological mental state. Indeed, we have no idea about whether the content of the delusion is too abnormal to be bimagined because we do not know what a normal bimagining is like. Bayne and Fernández (2009) make a similar point:

> Theorizing about delusion (and, to a lesser extent, self-deception) typically begins with the thought that these states are pathological beliefs – they violate certain norms of belief-formation. It is unclear how Egan's

account might accommodate this thought, for nothing can be a pathological belief unless it is also a belief.

(p. 17)

Egan might argue, however, that bimagination is an intrinsically pathological
mental category in the sense that all bimaginings are necessarily pathological.
Unlike other psychological categories such as the category of belief, there
is no distinction between pathological and non-pathological members of the
category of bimagination. All bimaginings are pathological simply by virtue of the fact that they belong to the category of bimagination. But why is
bimagination an intrinsically pathological category? One might think that it is
because bimaginings are intermediate states. But why are intermediate states
intrinsically pathological? There could be some intermediate mental states
that are not intrinsically pathological. For instance, Egan himself suggests that
self-deception involves an intermediate state with some belief-like features
and some desire-like features. But this intermediate category cannot be intrinsically pathological because self-deception is not intrinsically pathological.[19]

Egan introduces the category of bimagination through an analogy between
bimaginings and intermediate books with some fiction-like features and some
non-fiction-like features. But, this analogy misses something; there is nothing pathological, abnormal, or defective about the category of intermediate
books with some fiction-like and some non-fiction-like features (unless, for
example, there are some reasons to think that the intermediate category is aes-
thetically defective). Millikan (1989a) makes a similar point, using a similar
example, when talking about the normativity of the notion of defectiveness:

> Note how different the notion of 'defective' is from, say, 'borderline case'
> or the notion 'by courtesy'. Monographs may be only borderline cases of
> books, or may be books only by courtesy, but surely monographs are not
> defective books. The notion 'defective' is a normative notion.
>
> (p. 296)

I will come back to this issue in Chapter 3.

2.4 Compatibilism

2.4.1 *Doxastic function hypothesis*

I have examined incompatibilist options and raised some worries about
them. Now let us turn to the alternative option, namely the compatibilist option. In the rest of this chapter, I will show that teleo-functionalism
grounds an attractive compatibilist position.[20]

There are two claims, the weak claim and the strong claim, behind the view that teleo-functionalism grounds a compatibilist position. The weak claim is that, according to teleo-functionalism, DD and CDT are logically compatible with each other. It is not difficult to demonstrate this. According to teleo-functionalism, which says that beliefs are mental states with doxastic functions, DD is true if and only if the following is true:

Doxastic function hypothesis (DFH)

Delusions have doxastic functions.

Now, since CDT is perfectly compatible with DFH, it is also compatible with DD. Hence, DD and CDT are at least logically compatible with each other.

CDT is compatible with DFH because having doxastic functions is a historical property; a mental state has doxastic functions when it has the right kind of evolutionary history. And CDT, which is a thesis about the current causal property of delusions, is compatible with the possibility that delusions have the right kind of evolutionary history. Here is an analogy: Having the function of pumping blood is a historical property; a biological item has the function of pumping blood when it has the right kind of evolutionary history. Suppose that someone's diseased heart fails to behave like other hearts, e.g., it fails to pump blood properly. But the fact that the heart fails to behave like other hearts, which is a fact about the current causal property of the heart, is compatible with the possibility (which is indeed not just a possibility but rather the actualized one) that it has the right kind of evolutionary history.

The stronger and more interesting claim is that, according to teleo-functionalism, DD and CDT are not just logically compatible with each other but also true at the same time. In the following, I will give a defense of this claim. More precisely, my focus is on DD rather than CDT. (CDT will be assumed to be true in the following.) I will defend the claim that DD is true according to teleo-functionalism. The defense is a partial one because there are some open empirical issues that are relevant to evaluating the truth of DD in the teleo-functionalist framework.

Teleo-functionalism implies that DD is true if and only if DFH is true. Here is an important fact about DFH: We cannot simply argue that delusions do not have doxastic functions because they fail to actually perform them. Suppose, for example, what I called 'Ramseyanism' in Chapter 1 is true and, thus, doxastic functions are the functions of accurate-representing and action-guiding. Now, we cannot simply conclude that delusions do not have doxastic functions because delusions fail to accurately represent and fail to guide actions. To have the functions of accurate-representing and action-guiding is to have the right kind of history, and something can have the right kind of history without actually representing things accurately and guiding actions.

So, even if delusions fail to perform doxastic functions, it does not mean that DFH is false. Still, we do not yet have a reason to think that DFH is true. Providing such a reason is my task in what follows. The following discussions do not presuppose any specific conceptions of doxastic functions such as Ramseyanism. They only presuppose two general assumptions about doxastic functions.

The first assumption is that typical beliefs (i.e., the mental states that are typically referred to by the term 'beliefs') have doxastic functions. Any supporters of teleo-functionalism would want to accept this because the view turns out to be implausibly revisionist (i.e., typical beliefs turn out to be non-beliefs) if they reject this assumption. Indeed, this assumption is guaranteed to be true given what I said in Chapter 1 about the empirical exploration of doxastic functions. Doxastic functions are, in the process of scientific reduction, discovered empirically by investigating typical beliefs and their roles in evolutionary history. Therefore, given how the process of scientific reduction works, whatever doxastic functions are, it must be true that typical beliefs have doxastic functions.

The second assumption is that all of the statements about the functions of mental states are paraphrased into the statements about the functions of the mechanisms that produce the states in response to some inputs as well as the mechanisms that use the states to produce some outputs.

There is a theoretical reason to accept this assumption. So far, I have been assuming that functions can be attributed to mental states such as beliefs. This assumption is, strictly speaking, theoretically problematic because functions are attributed only to the items that are the products of natural selection. Mental states do not seem to satisfy this condition. On the one hand, I have a heart because my ancestors had hearts and they were selected. On the other hand, it is not the case, for example, that I believe that Toronto is cold in winter because my ancestors believed that Toronto was cold in winter, and the belief was selected. Godfrey-Smith (1989) nicely summarizes the problem when he talks about the functions of perceptual states:

> It is one thing to say that a mechanism has a biological function, and another to say that a particular state of the mechanism has a function. Eyes have evolved through natural selection, and have the function of picking up information in the form of light waves. Are particular states of this devise, ipso facto, functionally characterizable? . . . Structural features of the visual apparatus are products of an evolutionary history,

a history of heritable variation in fitness. But, states of visual system are not the right sort of things to have such a history. There exists no way their properties and powers can lead to there being future states of the same type (as opposed to states of a different type, not as opposed to no states at all).

(p. 542)

Following Millikan's (1984) suggestion, the problem can be solved by paraphrasing the statements about the functions of mental states into statements about the functions of the mechanisms that produce the mental states ('producers' in Millikan's terminology) and the ones that use the mental states ('consumers'). And the paraphrased statements are understood in the standard way in terms of the evolutionary history of the mechanisms. The statement that a mental state has doxastic functions is paraphrased into the statement that the producers and the consumers of the state have some corresponding functions. Let us call the functions that are attributed, in the paraphrased statements, to the producer mechanisms and the consumer mechanisms 'doxastic producer functions' and 'doxastic consumer functions' respectively. If accurate-representing is a doxastic function, for example, then producing accurate-representing states is a doxastic producer function.

Now, according to DFH, delusions have doxastic functions. With the second assumption, DFH might be paraphrased into the following:

Doxastic mechanism hypothesis (DMH)

Delusions are produced by the mechanisms with doxastic producer functions and are consumed by the mechanisms with doxastic consumer functions.

Let us assume for the moment that DMH is equivalent to DFH. (This assumption will be revised later in this chapter.) A problem with DFH, understood as it is, is that it does not give us a clear idea as to what needs to be done in order to test the claim. DMH, on the other hand, gives us a clear idea; we can test the claim empirically once we know, first, what mechanisms are producing and using delusional states and, second, what functions the mechanisms have. The relevant knowledge for this test seems to be empirically obtainable, at least in principle.

According to the first assumption, typical beliefs have doxastic functions, which is paraphrased, with the second assumption, into the claim that they are produced by the mechanisms with doxastic producer functions and consumed by the mechanisms with doxastic consumer functions. My general strategy for defending the claim that DD is true according to teleo-functionalism is to establish DMH by showing that delusions share the producers and consumers with typical beliefs. This implies that DFH, which is assumed to be equivalent to DMH, is correct, which in turn implies that DD is correct, according to teleo-functionalism. The reasoning goes like this:

(1) Typical beliefs are produced by the mechanisms with doxastic producer functions and consumed by the mechanisms with doxastic consumer functions. (= the first assumption, paraphrased)

(2) Delusions are (A) produced by exactly the same mechanisms that produce typical beliefs and (B) consumed by exactly the same mechanisms that consume typical beliefs.

(3) Therefore, delusions are produced by the mechanisms with doxastic producer functions and consumed by the mechanisms with doxastic consumer functions. (= DMH) [1 & 2]

(4) Delusions have doxastic functions. (= DFH, which is equivalent to DMH) [3]

(5) Beliefs are the mental states with doxastic functions. (= teleo-functionalism)

(6) Delusions are beliefs. [4 & 5]

Let us call (A) and (B) 'the same producer hypothesis' (SPH) and 'the same consumer hypothesis' (SCH) respectively. In what follows, I will provide some reasons to believe these hypotheses.

2.4.2 Same producer hypothesis

Let us begin with SPH. SPH is likely to be true about many delusions in light of what we already know about the delusion formation process. Arguably, one of the mechanisms that is responsible for the production of typical beliefs is the one that outputs beliefs in response to perceptual data. Let us call the mechanism P_B. (For the sake of simplicity, I am talking here as if P_B is a unitary mechanism. It would be more realistic to think that P_B is a collection of subsystems specializing in different types of tasks and processes.) The current empirical literature strongly suggests that many delusions are produced by P_B.

The empiricism about delusions is the view that delusions are formed in response to abnormal data.[21] There are different versions of empiricism. For example, one might think that abnormal data are sufficient for the formation of delusions (one-factor empiricism; e.g., Maher, 1974; see also Gerrans, 2002; Reimer, 2009) or, alternatively, that they are not (two-factor empiricism; e.g., Coltheart, 2007; Coltheart et al., 2011; Davies et al., 2001;

Langdon & Coltheart, 2000). In the former view, abnormal data are sufficient and, hence, anyone with the same abnormal data will, other things being equal, form delusions. In the latter view, in contrast, abnormal data are not sufficient and, hence, there could be, at least in principle, some people with the same abnormal data who do not form delusions.[22]

Ellis and Young (1990) propose an influential empiricist account of the Capgras delusion. According to their account, the Capgras delusion is caused by the disrupted connection between the face recognition system and the autonomic nervous system. This proposal is consistent with the finding of abnormal autonomic activities in people with the Capgras delusion (Ellis, Young, Quayle, & De Pauw, 1997). Because of the disruption, people with the Capgras delusion, when looking at a familiar face,

> receive a veridical image of the person they are looking at, which stimulates all the appropriate overt semantic data held about that person, but they lack another, possibly confirming, set of information which . . . may carry some sort of affective tone.
>
> (Ellis & Young, 1990, p. 244)

And the delusion is formed when the people respond to such an abnormal experience by adopting a 'rationalisation strategy in which the individual before them is deemed to be an imposter, a dummy, a robot, or whatever extant technology may suggest' (Ellis & Young, 1990, p. 244).

Kapur (2003) proposes an influential empiricist account of schizophrenic delusions. He argues that the abnormality in dopamine transmission in schizophrenia leads to an inappropriate attribution of salience, i.e., the attention-grabbing quality of events and objects.[23] Because of the inappropriate attribution of salience, banal events and objects all of a sudden grab attention and acquire special significance. A delusion is 'a "top-down" cognitive explanation that the individual imposes on these experiences of aberrant salience in an effort to make sense of them' (Kapur, 2003, p. 15). This hypothesis is coherent with the clinical observation that people with delusions in the context of schizophrenia often report that some events and objects have 'special meaning' for them, that they have an 'altered experience' of the world, that their awareness is 'sharpened', and so on.

Empiricism, which I will defend in Chapter 4, strongly suggests that many delusions are produced by P_B. My argument here is an inference-to-the-best-explanation argument. Many delusions are formed in response to abnormal data, according to empiricism. The best explanation of this is that these delusions are formed by P_B rather than by other mechanisms. According to empiricism, the Capgras delusion is formed in response to the abnormal data concerning familiar faces. The best explanation of this is that the Capgras delusion is produced by P_B.

Please note that the claim that many delusions are produced by P_B does not imply that P_B is functioning properly in producing them. For example, the two-factor empiricists might argue that P_B fails to perform its functions because it is damaged or biased. I will come back to this issue in Chapter 3.

2.4.3 Same consumer hypothesis

Let us now turn to SCH. Arguably, one of the mechanisms that is responsible for the consumption of typical beliefs is the one that initiates behavioral processes in response to beliefs and relevant motivational states. Let us call it C_B. (Again, C_B might be the collection of different mechanisms specializing in different tasks and processes.) The question for us, then, is whether or not delusions are consumed by C_B.

Unfortunately, we do not have enough empirical knowledge on this issue. So far, most empirical studies of delusions are about the causes of delusions. No systematic studies have been done about the effects of them. In other words, we do not know much about the delusion consumption processes. Still, it is a promising hypothesis that delusions are consumed by C_B. The main challenge to the hypothesis comes from the fact that some delusions fail to guide non-verbal actions. Why, if delusions are consumed by C_B, whose job is to initiate action-producing processes, do those delusions fail to guide non-verbal actions? Why, for instance, does a person with the Capgras delusion that his wife has been replaced by an imposter fail to act in accordance with the content of the delusion if the delusion is actually consumed by C_B?

There are at least two possible responses to this challenge. Consider the following analogy from Millikan (2004). There are at least two possible cases where a coffee machine fails to produce coffee even though I put coffee beans in it. In the first case, it fails to produce coffee because it is broken. (In my terminology in Chapter 3, the machine is 'malfunctioning' in this case.) In the second case, it fails to produce coffee not because it is broken but because I did not put water in it. (In my terminology, the machine is 'misfunctioning' in this case.)

Analogously, there are two possible explanations of the cases where a delusion fails to guide non-verbal actions despite the fact that the delusion is 'put in' C_B. In the first explanation, delusions are consumed by C_B but the mechanism fails to initiate appropriate behavioral processes because it is broken or damaged. This seems to be a perfectly coherent possibility.

In the second explanation, delusions are consumed by C_B but the mechanism fails to initiate appropriate behavioral processes, not because it is broken but because it does not receive other sorts of inputs, such as motivational inputs. Bortolotti and colleagues point out that this hypothesis is consistent with empirical evidence (Bortolotti, 2011; Bortolotti & Broome, 2012; Bortolotti & Miyazono, 2015; Miyazono & Bortolotti, 2014). For example, empirical evidence seems to suggest that people with delusions in the context of schizophrenia (1) lose the sense of genuine control over their own behavior that undermines the motivation to act, (2) fail to find the goal of action desirable, (3) have some general problems in producing self-willed action, (4) fail to find the goal of action attractive due to a flattening of affect (5) fail to enjoy the pleasant emotions associated with the goal of action, or (6) feel hopeless and pessimistic about the probability of achieving their goals due to emotional disturbances.[24]

2.4.4 Objections

I will now attend to some expected objections, and in particular objections to my inference-to-the-best-explanation argument for SPH.

> *Objection 1*: The argument for SPH does not cover all kinds of delusions because empiricism does not seem to be true of all kinds of delusions. For example, the delusion of jealousy (e.g., 'My husband is having an affair with his female secretary') does not seem to be formed in response to abnormal data. Even if abnormal data of some kind (such as abnormal salience attached to jealously inducing events) are involved in the formation of the delusion of jealousy, the role of the data does not seem to be as important as the role of the abnormal data for the Capgras delusion.

For those non-empirical delusions (i.e., delusions that cannot easily be explained by empiricism), separate arguments might be needed. The problem, however, is that the relevant empirical knowledge about non-empirical delusions is quite limited. We have relatively reliable empirical knowledge about empirical delusions (i.e., delusions that can easily be explained by empiricism), but we do not know as much about non-empirical ones. Still, some accounts of non-empirical delusions have been proposed, and SPH is consistent with the accounts. For example, according to Easton, Schipper, and Shackelford (2006, 2007), the delusion of jealousy is the product of the hypersensitivity of the evolved mechanism that is responsible for detecting a partner's infidelity. The same mechanism produces both normal jealousy and delusional jealousy, which is coherent with SPH. The difference is that, in the case of the delusion of jealousy, the mechanism becomes hypersensitive to the cues of infidelity and 'these individuals experience jealous reactions at a much lower threshold than normal individuals' (Easton et al., 2007, p. 399).

Again, one might think that motivated delusions, including the delusion in Reverse Othello syndrome (i.e., a delusion involving the idea of the fidelity of a romantic partner) and the delusion in erotomania (i.e., a delusion involving the idea that someone, typically with a high social rank or status, loves them), cannot be explained by empiricism. But they might be explained by a broadly empiricist account (e.g., McKay, Langdon, & Coltheart, 2005). Even if they are not, they might be understood as the exaggerated forms of everyday motivated beliefs,[25] which is consistent with SPH.

> *Objection 2*: Empiricism does not necessarily support SPH. Even if we accept the idea that delusions are formed in response to abnormal data, we could resist the idea that delusions are produced by P_B. Perhaps there are some other mechanisms that produce some other nondoxastic states in response to perceptual data. For example, Currie and Jureidini (2001) claim that imaginings are much more easily triggered by perception than beliefs. If this is correct, then probably there is a mechanism, P_I, which is distinct from P_B, that produces imaginings rather than beliefs in response to perceptual data. Then, we cannot rule out the hypothesis that delusions are produced by P_I rather than P_B even if empiricism is assumed to be true.

I agree that we cannot rule out the hypothesis that delusions are formed by P_I. Let us call this hypothesis 'the imagination producer hypothesis' (IPH). I do not think, however, that SPH and IPH are equally good hypotheses. A reason, which I already discussed above, is that, unlike imaginings, delusions do not seem to have the counterfactual openness to other possibilities. Unlike people who merely imagine something, people with delusions could not have easily adopted a different hypothesis with the perceptual data fixed. Another reason is that, on the one hand, in general P_B produces its outputs in such a way that the outputs are 'restricted' by the data, in the sense that the outputs can be viewed as the explanations of the data.[26] In the passages quoted earlier, for example, a delusion is regarded as a 'rationalisation strategy' (Ellis & Young, 1990) or 'a "top-down" cognitive explanation' (Kapur, 2003) of abnormal data. On the other hand, the same thing does not seem to be true of P_I. We certainly sometimes imagine something in response to perceptual data, but the relationship between data and outputs is often unrestricted. I might imagine, for example, the scenario in which I become the President of the United States of America while watching a live TV report on an inauguration ceremony. The hypothesis that I am the President of the United States of America is not restricted by what I am looking at;

the hypothesis is not an explanation of it. But then SPH is better than IPH at explaining the observation (O) that delusions are indeed restricted by the abnormal data; in the probabilistic form, $P(O|SPH) > P(O|IPH)$.[27]

> *Objection 3*: It is assumed in the discussion of Objection 2 that beliefs and imaginings are produced by different producer mechanisms: P_B and P_I. But what if this assumption is false? What if there are some mechanisms for multiple purposes such as the one for producing beliefs as well as imaginings? This possibility poses a challenge to the inference-to-the-best-explanation argument, which in effect tries to show that delusions are beliefs on the basis of the fact that they are produced by exactly the same mechanism that produces beliefs. Empiricism might suggest that delusions are produced by exactly the same mechanism that produces beliefs. But this does not imply that delusions are beliefs rather than imaginings if imaginings can also be produced by exactly the same mechanism.

In response to this objection, I first point out that it is perfectly possible, in the teleo-functionalist framework, that a mechanism has multiple functions. For the same reason that biological organs such as kidneys can have multiple functions, cognitive mechanisms can also have multiple functions. Now, I agree that there could be a mechanism that produces beliefs as well as imaginings.[28] However, it is likely that the relevant functions in producing beliefs (i.e., the functions that the mechanism attempts to perform when it produces beliefs) are different from the relevant functions in producing imaginings (i.e., the functions that the mechanism attempts to perform when it produces imaginings). The relevant functions in producing beliefs might include the function of, say, accurate-representing. Whatever these functions are, they are called 'doxastic producer functions' in my terminology. The relevant functions in producing imaginings might include the function of, say, enabling simulative processes, including counterfactual thinking, causal thinking, future planning, and mindreading. Whatever these functions are, we can call them 'imaginative producer functions'.

Suppose that delusions are produced by a mechanism with both doxastic and imaginative producer functions. One possible scenario is that delusions are produced when doxastic producer functions are relevant. Delusions should be regarded as beliefs in this scenario; the relevant functions in producing delusions are doxastic ones rather than imaginative ones. Another possible scenario is that delusions are produced when imaginative producer functions are relevant. Delusions should be regarded as imaginings in this scenario; the relevant functions in producing delusions are imaginative ones rather than doxastic ones.

My view is that the first scenario is more likely than the second scenario for the same reason that SPH is more plausible than IPH. The first is more likely than the second because delusions are restricted by the abnormal data, in the sense that they can be viewed as the explanations of the abnormal data.

So far, we have been assuming that DFH is equivalent to DMH. This assumption, however, needs to be revised in light of the foregoing discussion. The difference between the two scenarios above is crucial in evaluating the doxastic status of delusions. Delusions should be regarded as beliefs only in the first scenario. DMH, however, fails to distinguish the two scenarios. (The producer clause of) DMH is true in both scenarios; it is true in both scenarios that delusions are produced by the mechanism with doxastic producer functions. The problem can be fixed by revising DMH in the following way:

Doxastic mechanism hypothesis 2 (DMH2)

Delusions are produced by the mechanisms with doxastic producer functions when the doxastic producer functions are relevant and are consumed by the mechanisms with doxastic consumer functions when the doxastic consumer functions are relevant.

My proposal is that DFH is equivalent to DMH2, which does distinguish the two scenarios above. (The producer clause of) DMH2 is true only in the first scenario; it is true only in the first scenario that delusions are produced by the mechanism with doxastic producer functions when the doxastic producer functions are relevant.

2.4.5   *Delusions as in-between states?*

I have provided some reasons to accept SPH and SCH (although the reasons to accept the latter are weaker). If those hypotheses are true, then delusions are beliefs according to teleo-functionalism. I will close my discussion in this chapter with some remarks on the proposal by Egan and others that delusions are some in-between states, such as bimaginings.

Can delusions be bimaginings? This possibility cannot be ruled out, at least in dry-functionalist discussions. Dry-functionalism individuates mental states in terms of causal roles, and it is certainly possible that some states play some in-between, half-belief, half-imagining causal roles. As Egan (2009) points out, 'there seems to be no principled reason to think that we can't get a spectrum of cases, from clear, totally non-belief-like imaginings to clear, full-blooded, paradigmatic beliefs, with intermediate, hard-to-classify states in the middle' (p. 274) in the dry-functionalist classification of mental states. However, the situation is very different in the teleo-functionalist framework. There is a stark contrast between beliefs or imaginings on the one hand and bimaginings on the other. There is probably no room for bimagination as a *sui generis* mental state category, in which case the idea that delusions are bimaginings does not even get off the ground in the teleo-functionalist discussion.

Teleo-functionalism individuates mental states in terms of their functions, which means that all *sui generis* mental state categories need to be associated with some functions. On the one hand, teleo-functionalism recognizes belief and imagination as *sui generis* mental state categories because it is likely that beliefs and imaginings have some functions (or, more precisely, their producers and consumers have some functions). Perhaps the functions of beliefs are related to accurate-representing and action-guiding, and the functions of imaginings are related to simulative processes. On the other hand, teleo-functionalism does not recognize bimagination as a *sui generis* category because bimaginings do not seem to have any functions.

The following two conditions need to be met if bimaginings have some functions in the relevant sense (i.e., the etiological sense). First, bimaginings have some biologically useful effects. Second, bimaginings were selected for the useful effects. These conditions are, however, very unlikely to be met.

First, bimaginings do not seem to be biologically useful at all. It is certainly useful to have a mental state that accurately represents facts and guides actions. It is certainly useful to have a mental state that enables simulative processes. But it is very hard to see the biological advantage of having a mental state with some belief-like features and some imagining-like features. How can such a state enhance the chance of survival and reproduction?

Second, even if it turns out that bimaginings have biologically useful effects in some peculiar contexts (e.g., half-realistic, half-simulative processes), it is overwhelmingly likely that bimaginings have the effects accidentally, i.e., bimaginings were not selected for the effects. The idea that bimaginings were selected for some biological purposes, together with the view that delusions are bimaginings, seems to imply that delusions were selected for some biological purposes. Although this kind of adaptationist story has been proposed for some forms of mental disorders, current empirical research overwhelmingly supports the idea that delusion is not the product of past selection but is rather the product of some psychological and neuropsychological abnormalities, such as abnormal experiences, reasoning biases, dopamine dysregulations, and brain damages. This issue will be discussed in detail in Chapter 3.

Descartes argues in *The Passions of the Soul* that all *sui generis* emotions are useful for some purpose (but not in the biological sense): 'I cannot believe that nature has given to mankind any passion which is always vicious and has no good or praiseworthy function' (Descartes, 1985, p. 392). On the basis of this commitment, Descartes concludes that fear or terror are not *sui generis* emotions but rather an excess of other emotions: 'In the case of fear or terror, I do not see that it can ever be praiseworthy or useful. It, too, is not a specific passion, but merely an excess of timidity, wonder and anxiety' (Descartes, 1985, p. 392). Teleo-functionalists have a similar commitment that all *sui generis* mental states are biologically useful and that they were selected for their useful effects. Bimaginings do not seem to satisfy these conditions. But then, bimagination is not a *sui generis* mental state category but rather an 'excess' of other mental states such as beliefs or imaginings, i.e., the alleged bimaginings are in fact some abnormal beliefs or imaginings.

2.5 Summary

Recent philosophical debate on the nature question has been dominated by dry-functionalist discussions. The focus of the debate is on whether delusions play distinctive belief-like causal roles. Dry-functionalism is certainly a popular view (at least when it comes to beliefs and other propositional attitudes), but it is not 'the only game in town'. Teleo-functionalism is another form of functionalism with important theoretical motivations. In this chapter, I have provided a teleo-functionalist discussion of the nature question. The focus of my discussion has not been on whether delusions play distinctive belief-like causal roles but on whether they have distinctive belief-like functions.

According to the incompatibilist options (pro-DD incompatibilism and anti-DD incompatibilism), which are often associated with dry-functionalism, DD and CDT are incompatible with each other and thus at least one of them needs to be rejected. But there are some worries about the incompatibilist options. In contrast, teleo-functionalism grounds a compatibilist option according to which DD and CDT are compatible with each other. DD and CDT are at least logically compatible with each other according to teleo-functionalism and, moreover, there are some reasons to think that they (DD in particular) are true.

It is important to note that my discussions have been subject to certain limitations mainly due to the lack of relevant empirical knowledge. First, my discussion of SPH has mainly been about empirical delusions rather than non-empirical ones. Second, my discussion of SCH has mainly been about the producers of delusions rather than the consumers of them.

Notes

1 For example, Radden (2011) argues: 'Our category of belief may not accommodate all delusional states, true. But nor is that category precise enough, or sufficiently agreed upon, to exclude all delusions from the status of beliefs' (pp. 52–53).

2 The distinctions between different forms of DD might not be very sharp according to some theories of belief. For instance, the distinction between the attribution DD and the mental state DD would not be clear if we accept an interpretationist theory of belief, according to which the mental state of believing is constitutively linked to the practice of third-personal belief attribution. Again, the distinction between the concept DD and the attribution DD might not be very clear either if we take the view that the practice of third-personal belief attribution is constitutively linked to the application of the concept 'belief'. I do not rule out these views, but here I stick to the default assumption that they are at least *prima facie* distinct claims about *prima facie* distinct subject matters.

3 However, I do not deny that people with delusions sometimes get confused, lose confidence, etc. Delusions sometimes wax and wane (e.g., Coltheart, 2007). And, as Radden (2011) points out, 'subjective descriptions of both delusions and hallucinations are regularly accompanied by elaborate qualifications that echo these uncertainties over how to capture and represent such experiences' (p. 48).

4 But those who are sympathetic to the prediction-error theory of delusions tend to deny a sharp distinction between hallucination as a perceptual state and delusion as a doxastic state (e.g., Fletcher & Frith, 2009). The perceptual/doxastic distinction is not very clear according to the predictive coding (or the predictive processing) account of brain functions, which is the theoretical basis of the prediction-error theory. According to the predictive coding account, both perceptual and doxastic processes are understood in a unified manner as prediction-error minimization processes (e.g., Clark, 2013, 2016; Friston, 2005, 2010; Hohwy, 2013). See Chapter 4 for more details.

5 But there is a philosophical debate as to whether people with delusions really understand the meaning of the terms that are used to express their delusions. See, e.g., Bortolotti (2009, Chapter 2) and Campbell (2001).

6 Some delusions do have a significant impact on non-verbal actions, including violent actions. For the Capgras delusion and violent actions, see, e.g., de Pauw and Szulecka (1988) and Bourget and Whitehurst (2004).

7 In contrast, 'elaborated delusions' have a global impact on other beliefs. For instance, in the case mentioned above (Davies et al., 2001), the person with the delusion that he does not have any internal organs 'expressed the belief that spirit doctors had come to his room one night to perform a magical operation in order to remove his internal organs. This happened, he believed, because he was being punished by God for some evil or sin that he had committed, although he was uncertain about the nature of the sin' (p. 136). In this case, the original delusion about internal organs forces other beliefs to be revised, and the entire worldview of the person is infected by delusional ideas.

8 Again, this is not always that case. For instance, Christodoulou (1977) reports a case where a housewife, JD, with the Capgras delusion about her daughters 'refused to talk to her daughters and expressed fears that the "doubles" would poison her' (p. 557). He also reports another case where another housewife, PK, with the Capgras delusion about her husband 'reported to the police that her

husband had died and that an identical-looking man had taken his place. She put on black dress in mourning of her "late" husband, refused to sleep with his "double" and angrily ordered him out of the house, shouting "go to your own wife"' (p. 558).

9 See also Bayne and Pacherie (2005) and Reimer (2010a, 2010b).

10 See Reimer (2010a, 2010b) for a similar attempt: 'I defend the view in question against the argument that psychiatric delusions are not beliefs because they do not "act like" beliefs. Their comparatively weak influence on the subject's behavior, emotional life, and "web of beliefs" is not what one would expect from genuine beliefs. Additionally, psychiatric delusions tend to be intractable: resistant to counterevidence, however powerful. Ordinary beliefs, in contrast, tend to be rejected or at least revised in light of such evidence. In response to these considerations, I point out that what is said about psychiatric delusions might equally be said about other belief-like states whose epistemic status as beliefs is rarely questioned' (Reimer, 2010a, p. 317).

11 Perhaps the same thing is true of the imagination/supposition pair. Some philosophers draw a distinction between imagination and supposition (e.g., Gendler, 2000), but it is likely that the two categories are different only in degree, not in kind.

12 Or Bortolotti might argue that there are some non-delusional irrational beliefs with multiple delusional features (some religious beliefs?). But, then, we need to go back to the question (A) and ask if they are really beliefs rather than some other states.

13 See also Petrolini (2017).

14 Others argue that delusions are empty speech acts (Berrios, 1991), acceptances (Dub, 2017; Frankish, 2009), and perceptual inferences (Hohwy & Rajan, 2012). Stephens and Graham (2004) claim that being delusional is adopting a complex higher order attitude towards the lower order thought. But this view is (partly) compatible with DD view because the lower order thought can be a belief.

15 But Currie changed his view in a later paper (Currie & Jones, 2006), in which something like the bimagination account is defended. See the endnote 17 below.

16 'What is it for an imagining to be treated as if it were a belief, when in fact it is not one? What we suggest happens is this: The deluded subject fails to monitor the self-generatedness of her imagining that P. Because of this, her idea that P presents itself as something generated by the world beyond the self. In the kinds cases we are currently considering, it would be natural for it to seem that the idea that P is directly a response to the precipitating experience, as something peculiarly connected with and, hence, validated by the experience' (Currie & Jureidini, 2001, p. 160).

17 Currie and Jones (2006) express a similar view: 'Delusions . . . do not fit easily into rigid categories of either belief or imagination. While delusions generally have a significant power to command attention and generate affect, they vary a great deal in the extent to which they are acted upon and given credence by their possessors. In that case it may be that cognitive state do not sort themselves neatly into categorically distinct classes we should label "beliefs" and "imaginings", but that these categories represent vague clustering in a space that encompasses a continuum of states for some of which we have no commonly accepted labels' (p. 312).

18 For some objections to the imagination account, see, e.g., Bayne and Pacherie (2005). For some objections to the bimagination account and the in-between belief account, see, e.g., Bayne and Hattiangadi (2013).

19 Schwitzgebel's proposal faces the same problem because his other examples of in-between beliefs tend to be non-pathological (e.g., Schwitzgebel, 2001, 2002, 2010).

20 Bayne (2011) suggests a compatibilist option based on normative functionalism, and Clutton (2018) defends another compatibilist option based on a cognitive phenomenalist account. In his famous discussion of the mad pain case, Lewis (1983) considers a compatibilist account of pain based on a peculiar version of dry-functionalism.

21 The characterization of empiricism by Bayne and Pacherie (2004) is stronger. According to them, empiricism is committed to the 'bottom-up etiology thesis' (the proximal cause of the delusional belief is a highly unusual experience), the 'rationality thesis' (the delusional belief is a broadly rational response to the person's unusual experience), and the 'preservation of meaning thesis' (the words that are used to express delusional beliefs retain their usual meaning).

22 Another distinction is between 'endorsement empiricism' and 'explanation empiricism' (e.g., Bayne & Pacherie, 2004). According to the former, the delusion that P arises when a person endorses an abnormal experience with the content P or some other similar content. According to the latter, in contrast, the delusion that P arises when a person takes the hypothesis that P to be the best explanation of an abnormal experience with the content Q, where Q is 'thinner' or 'less precise' than P. The debate between explanation empiricism and endorsement empiricism is important, but for the sake of simplicity, my arguments simply presuppose explanation empiricism, which is more popular in the empirical literature. It should also be noted that the process of endorsement could be an extreme form of the process of explanation, where an experience with content P is explained by the hypothesis that P.

23 More precisely, the attribution of salience is 'a process whereby events and thoughts come to grab attention, drive action, and influence goal-directed behavior because of their association with reward or punishment' (Kapur, 2003, p. 14).

24 A limitation of this proposal is that the empirical evidence here comes from the research of schizophrenia. Delusions in non-schizophrenic contexts (e.g., the Capgras delusion due to brain injury) can fail to guide non-verbal actions as well (e.g., Stone & Young, 1997). Perhaps we need the first kind of explanation to account for these non-schizophrenic cases.

25 See Mele (2009) and Levy (2009) for the similarities between motivated delusion and (everyday) self-deception.

26 Here I assume the explanation empiricism. See endnote 22 above.

27 I do not deny that the outputs of P_I can be restricted by data in some cases. In the example by Currie and Jureidini (2001), for instance, I 'imagine that a stranger's gaunt appearance signals that he has AIDS' (p. 159). The hypothesis that he has AIDS does explain his gaunt appearance. But given the fact that these cases are relatively rare (i.e., rarer than the cases in which the outputs of P_B are restricted), this only shows that P(O|IPH) is not extremely low. It does not show that P(O|IPH) is as high as P(O|SPH).

28 There are some actual proposals of this kind. Nichols and Stich (2003) propose an architectural account of beliefs and imaginings according to which some mechanisms produce beliefs as well as imaginings. The same inference mechanism, for example, is responsible for producing beliefs as well as imaginings, which explains why imaginings exhibit the same kind of inferential regularities as beliefs do.

References

American Psychiatric Association. (2013). *Diagnostic and statistical manual of mental disorders* (5th ed.). Washington, DC: American Psychiatric Association.

Anselmetti, S., Cavallaro, R., Bechi, M., Angelone, S. M., Ermoli, E., Cocchi, F., & Smeraldi, E. (2007). Psychopathological and neuropsychological correlates of source monitoring impairment in schizophrenia. *Psychiatry Research, 150*(1), 51–59.

Bayne, T. (2011). Delusions as doxastic states: Contexts, compartments, and commitments. *Philosophy, Psychiatry, & Psychology, 17*(4), 329–333.

Bayne, T., & Fernández, J. (2009). Delusion and self-deception: Mapping the terrain. In T. Bayne & J. Fernández (Eds.), *Delusion and self-deception: Affective and motivational influences on belief formation* (pp. 1–21). Hove: Psychology Press.

Bayne, T., & Hattiangadi, A. (2013). Belief and its bedfellows. In N. Nottelmann (Ed.), *New essays on belief: Constitution, content and structure* (pp. 124–144). New York, NY: Palgrave Macmillan.

Bayne, T., & Pacherie, E. (2004). Bottom-up or top-down: Campbell's rationalist account of monothematic delusions. *Philosophy, Psychiatry, & Psychology, 11*(1), 1–11.

Bayne, T., & Pacherie, E. (2005). In defence of the doxastic conception of delusions. *Mind & Language, 20*(2), 163–188.

Berrios, G. E. (1991). Delusions as "wrong beliefs": A conceptual history. *The British Journal of Psychiatry, 159*(Suppl. 14), 6–13.

Bleuler, E. (1924). *Textbook of psychiatry* (trans. A. A. Brill). London: Allen and Unwin.

Bortolotti, L. (2009). *Delusions and other irrational beliefs*. New York, NY: Oxford University Press.

Bortolotti, L. (2011). Double bookkeeping in delusions: Explaining the gap between saying and doing. In J. Aguilar, A. Buckareff, & K. Frankish (Eds.), *New waves in the philosophy of action* (pp. 237–256). London: Palgrave Macmillan.

Bortolotti, L. (2012). In defence of modest doxasticism about delusions. *Neuroethics, 5*(1), 39–53.

Bortolotti, L., & Broome, M. R. (2012). Affective dimensions of the phenomenon of double bookkeeping in delusions. *Emotion Review, 4*(2), 187–191.

Bortolotti, L., & Miyazono, K. (2015). Recent work on the nature and development of delusions. *Philosophy Compass, 10*(9), 636–645.

Bourget, D., & Whitehurst, L. (2004). Capgras syndrome: A review of the neurophysiological correlates and presenting clinical features in cases involving physical violence. *The Canadian Journal of Psychiatry, 49*(11), 719–725.

Bovet, P., & Parnas, J. (1993). Schizophrenic delusions: A phenomenological approach. *Schizophrenia Bulletin, 19*(3), 579.

Brébion, G., Amador, X., David, A., Malaspina, D., Sharif, Z., & Gorman, J. M. (2000). Positive symptomatology and source-monitoring failure in schizophrenia: An analysis of symptom-specific effects. *Psychiatry Research, 95*(2), 119–131.

Campbell, J. (2001). Rationality, meaning, and the analysis of delusion. *Philosophy, Psychiatry, & Psychology, 8*(2), 89–100.

Christodoulou, G. N. (1977). The syndrome of Capgras. *The British Journal of Psychiatry, 130*(6), 556–564.

Clark, A. (2013). Whatever next? Predictive brains, situated agents, and the future of cognitive science. *The Behavioral and Brain Sciences, 36*(3), 181–204.

Clark, A. (2016). *Surfing uncertainty: Prediction, action, and the embodied mind.* New York, NY: Oxford University Press.

Clutton, P. (2018). A new defence of doxasticism about delusions: The cognitive phenomenological defence. *Mind & Language*, online first. Retrieved from https://doi.org/10.1111/mila.12164.

Coltheart, M. (2007). The 33rd Sir Frederick Bartlett Lecture: Cognitive neuropsychiatry and delusional belief. *The Quarterly Journal of Experimental Psychology, 60*(8), 1041–1062.

Coltheart, M., Langdon, R., & McKay, R. (2011). Delusional belief. *Annual Review of Psychology, 62*, 271–298.

Currie, G. (2000). Imagination, delusion and hallucinations. *Mind & Language, 15*(1), 168–183.

Currie, G., & Jones, N. (2006). McGinn on delusion and imagination. *Analytic Philosophy, 47*(4), 306–313.

Currie, G., & Jureidini, J. (2001). Delusion, rationality, empathy: Commentary on Martin Davies et al. *Philosophy, Psychiatry, & Psychology, 8*(2), 159–162.

Currie, G., & Ravenscroft, I. (2002). *Recreative minds: Imagination in philosophy and psychology.* New York, NY: Oxford University Press.

Davies, M., Coltheart, M., Langdon, R., & Breen, N. (2001). Monothematic delusions: Towards a two-factor account. *Philosophy, Psychiatry, & Psychology, 8*(2), 133–158.

De Pauw, K. W., & Szulecka, T. K. (1988). Dangerous delusions: Violence and the misidentification syndromes. *The British Journal of Psychiatry, 152*(1), 91–96.

Descartes, R. (1985). *The philosophical writings of Descartes* (Vol. 1, transl. J. Cottingham, R. Stoothoff, & D. Murdoch). Cambridge: Cambridge University Press.

Dub, R. (2017). Delusions, acceptances, and cognitive feelings. *Philosophy and Phenomenological Research, 94*(1), 27–60.

Easton, J. A., Schipper, L. D., & Shackelford, T. K. (2006). Why the adaptationist perspective must be considered: The example of morbid jealousy. *Behavioral and Brain Sciences, 29*(4), 411–412.

Easton, J. A., Schipper, L. D., & Shackelford, T. K. (2007). Morbid jealousy from an evolutionary psychological perspective. *Evolution and Human Behavior, 28*(6), 399–402.

Egan, A. (2009). Imagination, delusion, and self-deception. In T. Bayne & J. Fernández (Eds.), *Delusions and self-deception: Motivational and affective influences on belief formation* (pp. 263–280). Hove: Psychology Press.

Ellis, H. D., & Young, A. W. (1990). Accounting for delusional misidentifications. *The British Journal of Psychiatry, 157*(2), 239–248.

Ellis, H. D., Young, A. W., Quayle, A. H., & De Pauw, K. W. (1997). Reduced autonomic responses to faces in Capgras delusion. *Proceedings of the Royal Society of London B: Biological Sciences, 264*(1384), 1085–1092.

Fletcher, P. C., & Frith, C. D. (2009). Perceiving is believing: A Bayesian approach to explaining the positive symptoms of schizophrenia. *Nature Reviews Neuroscience*, *10*(1), 48.

Frankish, K. (2009). Delusions: A two-level framework. In M. R. Broome & L. Bortolotti (Eds.), *Psychiatry as cognitive neuroscience: Philosophical perspectives* (pp. 269–284). Oxford: Oxford University Press.

Friston, K. (2005). A theory of cortical responses. *Philosophical Transactions of the Royal Society B: Biological Sciences*, *360*(1456), 815–836.

Friston, K. (2010). The free-energy principle: A unified brain theory? *Nature Reviews Neuroscience*, *11*(2), 127.

Gendler, T. S. (2000). The puzzle of imaginative resistance. *The Journal of Philosophy*, *97*(2), 55–81.

Gerrans, P. (2002). A one-stage explanation of the Cotard delusion. *Philosophy, Psychiatry, & Psychology*, *9*(1), 47–53.

Godfrey-Smith, P. (1989). Misinformation. *Canadian Journal of Philosophy*, *19*(4), 533–550.

Hohwy, J. (2013). *The predictive mind*. New York, NY: Oxford University Press.

Hohwy, J., & Rajan, V. (2012). Delusions as forensically disturbing perceptual inferences. *Neuroethics*, *5*(1), 5–11.

Jenkinson, P. M., Edelstyn, N. M., Drakeford, J. L., & Ellis, S. J. (2009). Reality monitoring in anosognosia for hemiplegia. *Consciousness and Cognition*, *18*(2), 458–470.

Kapur, S. (2003). Psychosis as a state of aberrant salience: A framework linking biology, phenomenology, and pharmacology in schizophrenia. *American journal of Psychiatry*, *160*(1), 13–23.

Langdon, R., & Coltheart, M. (2000). The cognitive neuropsychology of delusions. *Mind & Language*, *15*(1), 184–218.

Levy, N. (2009). Self-deception without thought experiments. In T. Bayne & J. Fernández (Eds.), *Delusions and Self-deception: Motivational and Affective Influences on Belief Formation* (pp. 227–242). Hove: Psychology Press.

Lewis, D. (1983). Mad pain and Martian pain. In his *Philosophical Papers* (Vol. 1, pp. 122–129). New York, NY: Oxford University Press.

Lucchelli, F., & Spinnler, H. (2007). The case of lost Wilma: A clinical report of Capgras delusion. *Neurological Sciences*, *28*(4), 188–195.

Maher, B. A. (1974). Delusional thinking and perceptual disorder. *Journal of Individual Psychology*, *30*(1), 98–113.

McKay, R., & Cipolotti, L. (2007). Attributional style in a case of Cotard delusion. *Consciousness and Cognition*, *16*(2), 349–359.

McKay, R., Langdon, R., & Coltheart, M. (2005). "Sleights of mind": Delusions, defences, and self-deception. *Cognitive Neuropsychiatry*, *10*(4), 305–326.

Mele, A. (2009). Self-deception and delusions. In T. Bayne & J. Fernández (Eds.), *Delusions and self-deception: Motivational and affective influences on belief formation* (pp. 55–70). Hove: Psychology Press.

Millikan, R. G. (1984). *Language, thought, and other biological categories: New foundations for realism*. Cambridge, MA: The MIT Press.

Millikan, R. G. (1989). In defense of proper functions. *Philosophy of Science, 56*(2), 288.

Millikan, R. G. (2004). *Varieties of meaning: The 2002 Jean Nicod lectures.* Cambridge, MA: The MIT Press.

Miyazono, K., & Bortolotti, L. (2014). The causal role argument against doxasticism about delusions. *Avant: Trends in Interdisciplinary Studies, 5*(3), 30–50.

Nichols, S., & Stich, S. (2003). *Mindreading: An integrated account of pretence, self-awareness, and understanding other minds.* Oxford: Clarendon Press.

Petrolini, V. (2017). What makes delusions pathological *Philosophical Psychology, 30*(4), 502–523.

Radden, J. (2011). *On delusion.* London: Routledge.

Reimer, M. (2009). Is the impostor hypothesis really so preposterous? Understanding the Capgras experience. *Philosophical Psychology, 22*(6), 669–686.

Reimer, M. (2010a). Only a philosopher or a madman: Impractical delusions in philosophy and psychiatry. *Philosophy, Psychiatry, & Psychology, 17*(4), 315–328.

Reimer, M. (2010b). Distinguishing between the psychiatrically and philosophically deluded: Easier said than done. *Philosophy, Psychiatry, & Psychology, 17*(4), 341–346.

Schwitzgebel, E. (2001). In-between believing. *The Philosophical Quarterly, 51*(202), 76–82.

Schwitzgebel, E. (2002). A phenomenal, dispositional account of belief. *Noûs, 36*(2), 249–275.

Schwitzgebel, E. (2010). Acting contrary to our professed beliefs or the gulf between occurrent judgment and dispositional belief. *Pacific Philosophical Quarterly, 91*(4), 531–553.

Schwitzgebel, E. (2012). Mad belief? *Neuroethics, 5*(1), 13–17.

Schwitzgebel, E. (2015). Belief. In E. N. Zalta (Ed.), *The Stanford encyclopedia of philosophy* (Summer 2015 ed.). Retrieved from https://plato.stanford.edu/archives/sum2015/entries/belief/.

Stephens, G. L., & Graham, G. (2004). Reconceiving delusion. *International Review of Psychiatry, 16*(3), 236–241.

Stone, T., & Young, A. W. (1997). Delusions and brain injury: The philosophy and psychology of belief. *Mind & Language, 12*(3–4), 327–364.

Tumulty, M. (2011). Delusions and dispositionalism about belief. *Mind & Language, 26*(5), 596–628.

Tumulty, M. (2012). Delusions and not-quite-beliefs. *Neuroethics, 5*(1), 29–37.

3 Pathology

3.1 Overview

Delusions are pathological mental states, at least in typical cases. More precisely, they are pathological beliefs, assuming that DD is true. (And, for the sake of simplicity, I will assume that DD is true in this chapter.) Being pathological is not the same as being false or being irrational. Suppose that Anna falsely believes that her husband is having an affair. This belief might not be pathological; perhaps it is just a simple mistake. Suppose, again, that Sam irrationally believes, without good evidence, that he is smarter than his colleagues. This belief might not be pathological, either; perhaps it is just a non-pathological self-deception. But when a person with chronic schizophrenia believes that people look at her and gossip about her whenever she goes out in public (Case 1 in Chapter 1), or a person with brain damage believes that his father has been replaced by an imposter (Case 2 in Chapter 1), these beliefs are not merely false or irrational. They are pathological.

This chapter answers the pathology question, which is the question about what makes delusions pathological, distinguishing them from non-pathological false beliefs or irrational beliefs. The pathology question is closely related to the nature question in such a way that the answer to one question needs to be coherent with the answer to the other. But here is an apparent dilemma (which I already suggested in Chapter 2): On the nature question, you will either defend DD or reject it. If you defend DD, then you might emphasize the continuity between delusions and non-pathological beliefs. This is, for example, Bortolotti's (2009, 2012) view: 'There is continuity between everyday beliefs and clinical delusions. Clinical delusions are typically irrational to a greater extent or irrational across more dimensions than non-delusional beliefs, but they are irrational in roughly the same way' (Bortolotti, 2012, p. 39). But why are delusions pathological if they are continuous with non-delusional beliefs? What distinguishes pathological delusions from non-delusional beliefs? The job for the pro-DD theorists seems to be slightly tricky. On the one hand, they need to find the continuity between delusions and non-delusional beliefs in virtue of which delusions are included in the category of belief and, on the other hand, explain why delusions are pathological despite the continuity between them and non-delusional beliefs.

In contrast, if you reject DD, then you might emphasize the discontinuity between delusions and non-delusional beliefs. This is, for example, Egan's (2009) view: 'Categorizing delusions as straightforward cases of belief faces some pretty serious obstacles. The role that delusions play in their subjects' cognitive economies differs pretty dramatically from the role that we'd expect beliefs to play' (Egan, 2009, p. 266). But why are delusions pathological if they are discontinuous from non-delusional beliefs, such that they are excluded from the category of belief? Delusions are regarded as having a number of abnormal features, but these features are abnormal only against the background assumption that they are beliefs. For instance, the abnormal insensitivity to counterevidence is often regarded as an abnormal feature of delusions, but this feature is abnormal only against the background assumption that delusions are beliefs and thus they are supposed to be sensitive to evidence (including counterevidence). The job for the anti-DD theorists seems to be tricky, too, but for a different reason. On the one hand, they need to find the discontinuity between delusions and non-delusional beliefs in virtue of which delusions are excluded in the category of belief and, on the other hand, explain why delusions are pathological despite the lack of doxastic status.

So, our dilemma is this: Both the pro-DD theorists and the anti-DD theorists face tricky problems with respect to the pathology question. This chapter offers a solution to the dilemma. According to my proposal, which is a pro-DD one, delusions are continuous with non-delusional beliefs in one respect, which explains why they are included in the category of belief. At the same time, they are discontinuous from non-delusional beliefs in another respect, which explains why they are pathological. The continuity has something to do with the functions they have; delusions and non-delusional beliefs share the same functions ('doxastic functions'). This is what I argued in Chapter 2. The discontinuity has something to do with the failure of performing the functions;[1] unlike non-delusional beliefs, delusions fail to perform their functions.[2] (More precisely, delusions directly or indirectly involve some cognitive mechanisms that fail to perform their functions.) Delusions are, in my account, analogous to diseased hearts, which are continuous with healthy hearts in a respect (which explains why they are included in the category of heart) but are discontinuous from healthy ones in another respect (which explains why they are pathological). The continuity has something to do with the function they have; diseased hearts and healthy ones share the same function. The discontinuity has something to do with the failure to perform their function; unlike healthy hearts, diseased ones fail to perform their function.

The discussions in this chapter aim to clarify and defend this idea. First, I critically examine some possible answers to the pathology question (**3.2**). Then I argue, following Wakefield's harmful dysfunction analysis of disorder, that delusions are pathological because they involve some harmful malfunctions (**3.3**). An objection to the proposal is that delusions might not involve any malfunctions. Another objection is that a harmful malfunction is not sufficient for something to be pathological. These objections, however, should be rejected in the end (**3.4**).

Some clarifications are needed before going into the main discussions.

(1) The pathology question, which is about what makes delusions pathological, needs to be distinguished from a similar but different question about what makes delusional beliefs delusional. I will discuss the former, not the latter. The idea that a belief is pathological is different from the idea a belief is delusional. First, the delusionality of a belief might not imply its pathology.[3] There might be some delusional beliefs that are not pathological. Possible examples include the delusions (or delusion-like ideas) among non-clinical individuals (e.g., Freeman, 2006) and the delusion-like states that are induced by hypnosis (e.g., Connors et al., 2012). The pathology of a belief might not imply its delusionality, either. There might be some pathological beliefs that are not delusional. For example, some confabulations might be understood as non-delusional pathological beliefs.[4]

That said, I will refer to pathological delusions when I use the term 'delusions' in this chapter. And I will refer to non-delusional and non-pathological beliefs when I use the term 'non-delusional beliefs'.

(2) The pathology question does not necessarily presuppose a sharp boundary between delusions and non-delusional beliefs. Bortolotti and colleagues claim that delusions are in fact continuous with non-delusional beliefs (Bortolotti, 2009; Bortolotti, 2015; Bortolotti, Gunn, & Sullivan-Bissett, 2016; Sullivan-Bissett, Bortolotti, Broome, & Mameli, 2016). But it makes sense to ask why delusions are pathological even if there is no sharp boundary between delusions and non-delusional beliefs, for the same reason that it makes sense to ask why high blood pressure is dangerous even if there is no sharp boundary between high blood pressure and normal blood pressure.

3.2 Unsuccessful answers

(1) *Strangeness*: Anna's belief that her husband is having an affair is false, but the content of the belief is not very strange. Many married women can have a similar belief at some point. However, DS's belief that his father

was replaced by an imposter is both false and strange. This observation motivates the first proposal, according to which delusions are pathological because of their strange content. In other words, the pathology of a delusion comes from the abnormality of the content.[5]

A problem of this proposal is that it is not obvious that all delusions are significantly stranger than non-delusional beliefs. DS's belief is certainly strange, but there are some non-delusional beliefs that are as strange as his. For example, Murphy (2013) discusses a community in Sudan where it is believed that ebony trees provide important social information. The belief about ebony trees is culturally normal and hence not pathological. Nonetheless, it seems to be as strange as DS's delusional belief. One might think, however, that this problem can be solved by introducing a culture-relative notion of strangeness. The idea, for example, is that the belief about ebony trees is not strange relative to the cultural context in Sudan. DS's belief is strange relative to the western, modern cultural context to which he belongs. But this response does not solve all of the problems, because both pathological delusions and non-delusional beliefs with similar content can exist in the same cultural contexts. For example, it is difficult to distinguish Anna's belief from the delusion of jealousy by content alone, but they can be found in the same cultural context.

Another problem is that strangeness is not sufficient for a belief to be pathological. Philosophers seem to have strange beliefs (e.g., Reimer, 2010a, 2010b). For example, there are some philosophers who seriously believe: that every single object in the universe is conscious (panpsychism); that, for any object, however arbitrarily it is chosen, there is a further object that is composed by it (unrestricted composition); and that there are facts about the boundaries of a vague predicate which we can never discover (epistemicism about vague predicates). But, typically, these philosophical beliefs are not the expressions of a mental disorder but rather of remarkable insights and argumentative skills.

(2) *Irrationality*: Sam's belief that he is smarter than his colleagues is irrational, but DS's belief that his father was replaced by an imposter might be more irrational. Perhaps the latter is too irrational to be regarded as a non-pathological belief. According to the second proposal, delusion is pathological because of its extreme irrationality.[6]

It is not obvious, however, that delusional beliefs are extremely irrational. A worry about this proposal is that non-delusional beliefs can be irrational, too. For example, Bortolotti (2009, 2015) consistently argues that, when it comes to irrationality, delusional beliefs and non-delusional irrational beliefs are different only in degree, not in kind. Another worry is that delusional beliefs might not be so irrational. According to the empiricism about delusion formation, which I mentioned in Chapter 2 and will discuss in more depth in Chapter 4, delusions are formed in response to abnormal data. And some empiricists maintain that adopting a delusional hypothesis is a reasonable response to abnormal data (e.g., Coltheart, Menzies, & Sutton, 2010; Maher, 1974).

Other empiricists, however, are skeptical about the view that a delusion is a reasonable response to abnormal data. Stone and Young (1997), for instance, argue that the process of delusion formation is irrational because of 'the bias towards observational adequacy'; people with delusions irrationally place more emphasis on incorporating new observations into their belief system ('observational adequacy') than keeping their existing beliefs as long as possible ('doxastic conservatism'). McKay (2012) follows this suggestion and turns it into a mathematical hypothesis, according to which delusional beliefs are produced through the Bayesian-irrational reasoning process with the bias of discounting prior probabilities; people with delusions irrationally place more emphasis on likelihoods (which summarize how nicely hypotheses explain the observation) than prior probabilities (which summarize how probable the hypotheses are prior to the observation). But even if Stone, Young, and McKay are correct (and I do argue that they are correct in Chapter 4), it is still not obvious that delusional beliefs are extremely irrational, because the first worry still remains; similar irrational biases might be found in normal belief formation processes. For example, the famous study by Kahneman and Tversky (1973) on base-rate neglect shows that there is a widespread tendency to neglect the base-rate information that is relevant to relevant hypotheses. As Kahneman and Tversky point out, this tendency to neglect the base-rate information amounts to the tendency to neglect prior probabilities because the base-rate information in the experiment gives the prior probabilities of the relevant hypotheses.[7]

(3) *Understandability*: Sam's belief that he is smarter than his colleagues is irrational, but it is 'understandable' in the sense that we can give a simple folk psychological account of the belief. Sam comes to believe it because he wants it to be the case that he is smarter than his colleagues. In other words, his belief is driven by the desire to be smarter than his colleagues. In contrast, DS's belief that his father was replaced by an imposter is not 'understandable' in this way. There are no easy folk psychological explanations of DS's delusional belief. According to the third proposal, delusions are pathological because of the 'ununderstandability', which is understood as the resistance to folk psychological explanations.[8]

This proposal, however, is not fully satisfactory. First, it is not clear that the all delusions resist folk psychological explanations. Sam's belief is 'understandable' because we can identify the motivational factors that play crucial roles in the formation of the belief. But, then, at least motivated delusions are 'understandable' in the same way, by identifying the motivational factors.[9] Butler (2000) reported the case of B.X. who had delusional beliefs due to Reverse Othello syndrome. B.X. was a gifted musician who had been left quadriplegic following a car accident. One year after his injury, he developed delusional beliefs about the continuing fidelity of his former romantic partner, N., who had in fact severed all contact with him soon after the accident. A straightforward folk psychological explanation of this case would be that B.X. formed his delusional beliefs because he desperately wanted it to be the case that N. still loved him. In other words, his delusional beliefs were driven by the desire that N. still loved him.

Second, resisting folk psychological explanations does not seem to be sufficient for beliefs, or mental states in general, to be pathological. The so-called twisted self-deception is a good example. Twisted self-deceptive beliefs are, roughly speaking, unwelcome irrational beliefs. For example, if it turns out that Anna's belief about her husband's affair is not supported by the available evidence, it is a twisted self-deceptive belief. Presumably there is no straightforward folk psychological explanation of twisted self-deceptive beliefs. Mele (1999) provides an influential account according to which twisted self-deceptive beliefs are explained by people's tendency to avoid costly errors. If, on the one hand, Anna falsely believes that her husband is having an affair, then the falsity is not very costly; it only annoys her husband. If, on the other hand, she falsely believes that her husband is not having an affair, then the falsity is very costly; their marriage is seriously threatened. The twisted self-deceptive belief is the product of a process that avoids the latter kind of errors, which are very costly. Note that this account is not a folk psychological one. The idea that people choose their beliefs so that they can avoid costly errors does not seem to be a part of folk psychology. Indeed, the account relies on the scientific, not folk, psychological model of hypothesis testing by Friedrich (1993).

Another example comes from Gendler's (2008) discussion of aliefs. People experience an extreme fear when they walk on the transparent walkway 4000 feet above the floor of the Grand Canyon. There is nothing abnormal or pathological in this experience. As Gendler (2008) notes, 'the basic phenomenon – that stepping onto a high transparent safe surface can induce feelings of vertigo – is both familiar and unmysterious' (p. 635). Nonetheless, explaining the extreme fear is not very easy. The people who walk on the walkway seem to believe that the walkway is safe. But then why do they feel extreme fear? The fear is very mysterious if they seriously believe that the walkway is safe. Are they, then, somewhat skeptical about the safety? In that case, however, we cannot explain the fact that they step onto the walkway in the first place; 'no one would willingly step onto a mile-high platform if they had even a scintilla of doubt concerning its stability' (Gendler, 2008, p. 635). Presumably there is no folk psychological explanation of this case. Gendler argues that they feel extreme fear because they alieve that the walkway is not safe, although they believe that it is safe. An alief is, according to Gendler, 'a mental state with associatively linked content that is representational, affective and behavioral, and that is activated – consciously or nonconsciously – by features of the subject's internal or ambient environment' (Gendler, 2008, p. 645). Although 'alief' sounds like another folk psychological category, Gendler's account should not be understood as a folk psychological one. After all, alief is not a part of the conceptual repertoire of folk psychology. Perhaps her account is best understood as an extended folk psychological account.[10]

(4) *Responsibility*: Suppose that Anna, on the basis of her belief, acts violently to the woman who is mistakenly regarded as the woman with whom her husband is having an affair. The falsity of the belief does not change the fact that Anna is responsible for what she does. Anna is clearly responsible for her violence. However, if DS had acted violently to his father because of his delusional belief, he would not have been fully responsible for the violence. The fourth proposal is that delusions are pathological because responsibility-grounding capacities (such as decision-making capacity or self-regulating capacity) are significantly impaired in people with delusions.

An immediate problem is that this proposal does not explain why only some specific mental states, namely delusions (and perhaps some other abnormal states), are pathological but others are not. Suppose that responsibility-grounding capacities were indeed impaired in the case of DS. What explains the fact that only some specific mental states – such as his delusional belief about the identity of his father – are pathological, but other states – such as his non-delusional beliefs (e.g., his belief that Paris is the capital of France), desires (e.g., his desire for Thai food), and emotions (e.g., his fear of snakes) – are not?

Another problem is that it is far from obvious that responsibility-grounding capacities are always impaired in people with delusions. Certainly, it is likely that belief-forming capacity is impaired in one way or another (which will be the main topic of Chapter 4). However, the impairment of belief-forming capacity does not imply the impairment of responsibility-grounding capacities.

A possible response to this challenge is that belief-forming capacity is relevant in the context of the attribution of responsibility. In other words, responsibility-grounding capacities include belief-forming capacity. For example, according to the M'Naghten rule, a person is not responsible for what he does when he is ignorant of 'the nature and quality of the act he was doing'. Presumably people with delusions are ignorant of the nature and quality of their acts because of the impaired belief-forming capacity, and this explains why they are not responsible for their actions. However, this response is not very convincing. There is certainly a sense in which a violent person with the Capgras delusion is ignorant of the nature and quality of his act; he thinks that he is attacking the imposter, which is false. But this is also true about Anna; she thinks that she is attacking the woman with whom her husband is having an affair, which is false. So, if the phrase 'being ignorant of the nature and quality of acts' means 'having the false belief about the acts' or 'not having the true belief about them', then Anna is as ignorant as the person with the Capgras delusion.

Another response is that the delusion is just the tip of the iceberg. People with delusions often have other kinds of abnormalities at the same time, and these abnormalities impair responsibility-grounding capacities. For instance, delusions in the context of schizophrenia are accompanied by other positive and negative symptoms that could directly or indirectly impair responsibility-grounding capacities. However, we cannot assume *a priori* that responsibility-grounding capacities are always compromised in people with schizophrenia. Given the fact that schizophrenia is an extremely heterogeneous condition, we should probably expect large individual differences among people with schizophrenia when it comes to the quality of responsibility-grounding capacities. As Bortolotti, Broome, and Mameli (2014) point out, the fact that a person receives the diagnosis of schizophrenia might not, in itself, tell us much about his responsibility-grounding capacities:[11]

> The assumption that people who have psychotic symptoms or have received a diagnosis of schizophrenia lack responsibility or have reduced responsibility for action is especially problematic, as the behavior of two people with psychosis or schizophrenia can differ almost entirely. Some people with schizophrenia are able to function well, cognitively and socially, and to control their delusions to some extent
>
> (p. 379)

3.3   Harmful dysfunction analysis and delusion

The main problem of the previous proposals is that they are detached from the considerations about what, in general, makes a condition pathological. In order to explain why condition X is pathological, first, we need to have a general account of the features that make something pathological, and, second, we need to show that X has those features. However, the previous proposals skip the first step and simply point out some salient features of delusions. This invites all sorts of counterexamples and difficulties.

Wakefield (1992a, 1992b) presented a general account of disorder, which is very influential and, in my view, more plausible than its rivals. It is often called 'harmful dysfunction analysis of disorder' (HDA, hereafter). According to HDA, disorders are 'harmful dysfunctions' or 'harmful malfunctions'. Being 'harmful' means having a negative impact on well-being. The harmfulness condition is necessary because 'disorder is in certain respects a practical concept that is supposed to pick out only conditions that are undesirable and grounds for social concern' (Wakefield, 1992b, p. 237). A 'dysfunction' or 'malfunction' is the failure to perform functions.[12] For instance, a heart malfunctions when it fails to pump blood, a kidney malfunctions when it fails to filter metabolic waste from blood, a corpus callosum malfunctions when it fails to facilitate interhemispheric communications, and so on.

My proposal, which relies on HDA, is that delusions are pathological because (A) they are harmful and (B) they are malfunctional in the sense that they involve some malfunctioning cognitive mechanisms directly or indirectly. I will call (A) and (B) 'the harmfulness thesis' and 'the malfunction thesis' respectively. This proposal is at least partially consistent with Bortolotti's (2009) suggestion that the pathology of delusions has something to do with their harmful impact on well-being. According to HDA, however, it also has something to do with their malfunctional nature.

HDA is a controversial view. It is not my purpose in this chapter to defend HDA from the objections to it. It should be noted, however, that most (if not all) objections are aimed at refuting the necessity claim of HDA, namely, the claim that a harmful malfunction is necessary for a disorder. In contrast, what is crucial for my account is the idea that a harmful malfunction is sufficient for a disorder.[13]

For example, Tengland (2001) argues that viral infection is a counterexample to HDA. Viral infection is a disorder, but its symptoms (e.g., fever, cough, sneezing) are often biological defenses, not malfunctions. Murphy and Woolfolk (2000) point out that appendicitis is another counterexample. Appendicitis is clearly a disorder, but vestigial organs, such as the appendix, cannot fail to perform their functions because they do not have functions in the first place. Wakefield argues, in response to Tengland, that viral infection involves malfunctions at the cellular level (Wakefield, 2011) and, in response to Murphy and Woolfolk, that appendicitis involves malfunctions at the tissue level (Wakefield, 2000). In my opinion, Wakefield's responses are convincing. But, even if they are not, those counterexamples are the ones to the necessity claim of HDA rather than to the sufficiency claim.[14]

The harmfulness thesis: Some clarificatory remarks on the harmfulness thesis are in order. First, the 'harm' at issue does not have to be the harm to people with delusions themselves. It might be the harm to people around them, such as family members, friends, colleagues, or neighbors. It is conceivable that some people with delusions are happy precisely because of their delusions. For example, a person with the delusion of grandeur about special abilities given to them by God might be happy because of the delusion. Still, the delusion might cause some consequences that are harmful to those around the person.

Second, delusions might cause harmful consequences to the person without his being aware of it. For example, the delusion of grandeur might prevent a person from having a fulfilling social or work life without his being aware of the nature of the problem.[15] Relatedly, the harmful aspect of delusions might not be captured in terms of hedonistic factors such as pains and pleasures. Living in the experience machine (where one floats about in a tank in a laboratory, connected to the machine that produces the perfect illusion of leading whatever kind of life one desires) is extremely pleasurable from the hedonistic point of view, but many (perhaps most) people have the intuition that living in the machine is not very attractive (Nozick, 1974). Similarly, it is conceivable that living with the delusion of grandeur about special abilities is pleasurable, at least for a while, from the hedonistic point of view, but such a life might not be very attractive.[16]

Third, there is an implicit *ceteris paribus* clause in the harmfulness thesis. Delusions are *ceteris paribus* harmful, which is consistent with the possibility that some delusions turn out to be beneficial out of sheer luck. For example, we can imagine a case in which a person avoided a fatal plane crash because he had changed the reservation due to his delusional belief that a secret organization wanted him to do so. In this case, his delusional belief is beneficial rather than harmful. The same thing is true about disorders in general. For example, we can easily imagine the case in which the person avoided the plane crash because he had changed his reservation because of the flu. But, of course, this case does not show that having the flu is not a harmful condition. The claim that having the flu is harmful has an implicit *ceteris paribus* clause, and these unusual cases do not contradict the *ceteris paribus* claim.

The malfunction thesis: According to the malfunction thesis, delusions are malfunctional in the sense that they involve some malfunctions directly or indirectly. Delusions involve malfunctioning mechanisms directly when belief-forming mechanisms are malfunctioning. They involve malfunctioning mechanisms indirectly when some other mechanisms that are causally related to belief-forming mechanisms (e.g., perceptual mechanisms) are malfunctioning. At the moment, the malfunction thesis is somewhat speculative. We do not know the nature of the malfunctions yet because we do not yet have the complete picture of what goes on in the minds of people with delusions. Nonetheless, our current understanding of the process of delusion formation is informative enough for making some educated guesses.

According to empiricism, for example, delusions are formed in response to abnormal data. A hypothesis is that the abnormal data are malfunctional, i.e., the data are produced by some malfunctioning mechanisms. Delusions involve malfunctioning mechanisms indirectly in this case. This hypothesis is consistent with the standard theory of the Capgras delusion (e.g., Ellis & Young, 1990; Stone & Young, 1997), according to which the Capgras delusion is formed in response to the abnormal data generated by the disconnection between the autonomic nervous system and the face recognition system.[17] Another hypothesis is that not only the abnormal data but also the responses to them are malfunctional, i.e., P_B (i.e., which is the mechanism that outputs beliefs in response to perceptual data) is malfunctioning.[18] Delusions involve malfunctioning mechanisms directly in this case. This hypothesis is equivalent to the idea that delusions are what McKay and Dennett (2009) call 'doxastic dysfunctions':

> [Delusional] misbeliefs result from breakdowns in the machinery of belief formation. If we conceive of the belief formation system as an information processing system that takes certain inputs (e.g., perceptual inputs) and (via manipulations of these inputs) produces certain outputs (beliefs, e.g., beliefs about the environment that the perceptual apparatus is directed upon), then these misbeliefs arise from dysfunction in the system – doxastic dysfunction. Such misbeliefs are the faulty output of a disordered, defective, abnormal cognitive system.
>
> (p. 496)

I will defend an empiricist account of delusion formation in Chapter 4, which provides a clearer picture of malfunctions that are present in people with a delusion.

3.4   Objections

3.4.1   *Delusions are not malfunctional*

There are at least two kinds of possible objections to the claim that delusions are pathological because of X. First, there might be some objections according to which it is not the case that all delusions are X (or, more precisely, all pathological delusions are X). For example, an objection to the view that delusions are pathological because of their strangeness is that it is not the case that all delusions are strange (or, more precisely, all pathological delusions are strange). The delusion of jealousy is not strange, for example. Second, there might be some objections according to which X is not sufficient for a belief to be pathological. For example, an objection to the view that delusions are pathological because of the resistance to folk psychological explanations is that resisting folk psychological explanations is not sufficient for a belief to be pathological. Twisted self-deceptive beliefs resist folk psychological explanations, but they are not (always) pathological.

In this section, I examine two kinds of objections to my own proposal. According to the first group of objections (**3.4.1**), it is not the case that all delusions are malfunctional. Some of them are perfectly functional. According to the second group of objections (**3.4.2**), a harmful malfunction is not sufficient for a belief to be pathological. There are some beliefs that are harmful and malfunctional but not pathological.

Psychological defense: One might think that some delusions are not malfunctional at all; they are successfully performing a psychological defense function. In the case of B.X. that I mentioned above, for instance, his delusion about the fidelity of N. performs the psychological defense function; it defends B.X. from the devastating reality that his body was paralyzed and N. did not love him anymore. Indeed, it is a popular idea that some delusions play defensive roles (e.g., McKay, Langdon, & Coltheart, 2005).

This objection should be rejected because it rests on the confusion between 'functions' in the etiological sense and 'functions' in the psychological sense. I do not rule out the idea that some delusions perform a psychological defense function. But performing a psychological function is not the same as performing an etiological function. For example, defending self-esteem is psychologically beneficial (i.e., enhancing psychological happiness). But it is unclear that defending self-esteem is not only psychologically beneficial but also etiologically or biologically beneficial (i.e., enhancing fitness).

Psychological benefits and etiological benefits can come apart. For example, negative emotions, such as fear or anxiety, are psychologically detrimental, but they are etiologically beneficial (e.g., for avoiding dangers or threats). We might even say that negative emotions are etiologically beneficial because they are psychologically detrimental; they would not have been useful for avoiding dangers or threats if they had been psychologically beneficial. Furthermore, there are some conditions that are psychologically beneficial but etiologically detrimental. For example, Nesse (1998) argues that insufficient anxiety, which is psychologically beneficial, is etiologically detrimental. Anxiety has important etiological functions (e.g., making us prepared for future risks and dangers). Insufficient anxiety is an etiologically detrimental condition in which these etiological functions fail to be performed.

Doxastic shear pin: McKay and Dennett (2009) consider an interesting hypothesis according to which delusions involve what they call 'doxastic shear pins'. A shear pin is a metal pin installed in complex mechanistic systems, and it is designed to break in certain circumstances in order to prevent more serious consequences, such as the breakdown of other, more expensive parts of the systems. It is conceivable that some delusions are the product of something like a shear pin breakage. A possible hypothesis is that there is a mechanism whose normal function is to prevent motivational factors from influencing belief formation processes. Just like a shear pin, however, the mechanism is designed to break in the situation where one faces extreme psychological stress, letting motivational factors influence belief formation processes in order to prevent more serious consequences, such as a devastating cognitive or agential breakdown. For example, the mechanism might be broken in the case of B.X., in accordance with the design, in the face of the extreme psychological stress, thus letting motivational factors such as his desire for the continuing fidelity of N. influence belief formation processes in order to prevent more serious consequences.

Mishara and Corlett (2009) propose another version of the shear pin hypothesis based on the prediction-error theory (which I will explain in detail in Chapter 4). Due to aberrant prediction-error signals, trivial objects or events become abnormally salient and attention-grabbing (e.g., Kapur, 2003). This is what happens at the early stage of the so-called delusional mood. A delusion arises as the explanation of the abnormal salience attached to the objects and events. Just like a shear pin breaks in order to protect expensive parts, a delusion arises in order to reorganize 'the patient's experience to maintain behavioral interaction with the environment despite the underlying disruption to perceptual binding processes' (Mishara & Corlett, 2009, p. 531).[19]

I do not have *a priori* reasons to rule out these hypotheses. What is crucial for me is that they are perfectly compatible with my proposal. They are compatible because there might be some malfunctions that are directly or indirectly related to delusional beliefs even if one of these hypotheses turns out to be true. This is likely in Mishara and Corlett's hypothesis, in which it is assumed that prediction-error signaling is hypothesized to be abnormal, causing abnormalities in attention-allocation processes. In the hypothesis considered by McKay and Dennett, the mechanism that normally constrains the influence of motivational factors on belief formation fails to perform its normal function. After all, the mechanism is broken, just like a broken shear pin. It is certainly true that it successfully performs another function, namely, the function of preventing more serious consequences. But it does so by failing to perform its normal function. Presumably, the mechanism is best understood as having two incompatible functions. On the one hand, it has the (normal) function of constraining the influence of motivational factors on the belief formation processes. On the other hand, it has the (abnormal) function of preventing more serious consequences. Those functions are incompatible because the mechanism successfully performs the latter function only by failing to perform the former (and *vice versa*). When the 'shear pin' breaks, the mechanism is functional in the sense that it successfully performs the latter function, but it is malfunctional in the sense that it fails to perform the former.

The error management theory: This theory (Haselton & Buss, 2000) holds that recurrent asymmetries in the costs of false alarms shape a variety of cognitive and behavioral biases over evolutionary history. For example, the sexual overestimation bias (i.e., men's tendency to overperceive women's sexual interest) is explained by the recurrent asymmetry in the costs of errors. Smoke detectors are designed to activate more often than they really need to. This is because false positives are not very costly (i.e., there are some unnecessary evacuations), while false negatives are extremely costly (i.e., the building will be burnt down). Similarly, natural selection has designed the male sexual perception system so that it is activated more often than it really needs to be:

> False alarms typically result in trivial expenditures of wasted courtship effort for men: Although rejected men may experience social embarrassment, women generally do not respond antagonistically to men's overperception of sexual interest. The costs of missed mating opportunities, on the other hand, were substantial for men over the course of human evolution, because men's reproductive success can be directly affected by the access to fertile mates.
>
> (Perilloux, Easton, & Buss, 2012, p. 146)

Some might think that the error management theory causes a serious problem for my proposal; some delusions might be produced by the error management theoretic biases that evolved due to recurrent cost asymmetries. The biases are not malfunctional; they arise due to the design of relevant mechanisms. The delusion of jealousy is a good target for an error management theoretic account. False positives about the infidelity of one's partner do not seem to be very costly (i.e., their partner will be annoyed), while false negatives are very costly (i.e., their partner might leave them). So, the error management theory predicts that jealousy is, by design, activated more often than it needs to be. In other words, people are designed to be oversensitive to the infidelity of one's partner. It is conceivable that this bias explains both normal and delusional jealousy. Indeed, delusional jealousy seems to have some important characteristics in common with normal jealousy. For instance, men with delusional jealousy are especially upset about their partner's sexual infidelity, whereas women with delusional jealousy are especially upset about their partner's emotional infidelity, which is consistent with the pattern that is seen in normal jealousy (Easton et al., 2007). If it is true that the delusion of jealousy is the product of the error management theoretic bias, then there is nothing malfunctional about the delusion. Indeed, Easton and colleagues suggested that 'morbid jealousy does not meet the dysfunction criterion and therefore should not be considered a mental disorder' (Easton et al., 2006, p. 412).

The error management theory is a very plausible view. But if the theory is true, it does not cause any serious trouble for my account. First, perhaps Easton and colleagues are simply correct when they claim that the delusion of jealousy is not a pathological condition. And this is perfectly consistent with my proposal. As I already noted, it is not my claim that all delusions are pathological. My claim is rather that delusions are pathological, when they are in fact pathological, because they involve some harmful malfunctions.

Second, the delusion of jealousy might be pathological in the same way that a fever (as a symptom of viral infection) is pathological. A fever as a symptom of viral infection itself is not malfunctional; it is a designed defensive response. When we regard a fever as pathological, we do so in virtue of the fact that it is a symptom of viral infection, which involves malfunctions. In other words, a fever indirectly involves malfunctions even though it is perfectly functional. The same thing might be true about the delusion of jealousy. Indeed, the delusion of jealousy often occurs as a symptom of the conditions that are likely to involve some malfunctions. It occurs, for example, in the contexts of schizophrenia, bipolar disorder, Parkinson's disease, brain injuries, and so on. When we regard the delusion of jealousy as pathological in those contexts, we do so presumably in virtue of the fact that it is a symptom of the conditions that involve malfunctions. The delusion of jealousy, then, indirectly involves malfunctions even if it is perfectly functional.

Third, even if non-clinical people have the error management theoretic bias of being oversensitive to the infidelity of their partner, the bias might not be sufficient to explain the delusion of jealousy. A possibility is that the bias is pathologically exaggerated in people with the delusion of jealousy. McKay and Dennett (2009) suggest such a possibility:

> The most that can presently be claimed is that delusions may be produced by extreme versions of systems that have evolved in accordance with error management principles, that is, evolved so as to exploit recurrent cost asymmetries. As extreme versions, however, there is every chance that such systems manage errors in maladaptive fashion.
>
> (p. 502)

Indeed, if the delusion of jealousy is just an expression of an error management theoretic bias, how do we explain the fact that it can be seen in the context of schizophrenia or brain injuries? Presumably, the delusion of jealousy is more similar to rheumatoid arthritis, which is the product of pathologically exaggerated immune responses, than to a fever in viral infection. Another possibility is that the error management theoretic bias is only a factor of delusional jealousy. As we will see in Chapter 4, there can be multiple causal factors in the delusion formation process, and this could also be true about the delusion of jealousy. It is conceivable that the error management theoretic bias is just a factor, which, in causing the delusion, requires some other causal factors that involve some malfunctions.[20]

3.4.2   Harmful malfunction is not sufficient

According to the second objection, a harmful malfunction is not sufficient for a belief to be pathological. A version of this objection goes as follows. It is sometimes said that the fundamental idea of teleosemantics is that misrepresentations, such as non-veridical perceptions or false beliefs, involve the failure of functions. In the passage by Millikan (2004) that I quoted in Chapter 1, for example, she says that false representations 'are "representations" in the sense that the biological function of the cognitive systems that made them was to make them represent things. Falsehood is thus explained by the fact that purposes often go unfulfilled' (pp. 64–65).[21] But if this means that all misrepresentations involve malfunctions, then, according to my proposal, all harmful misrepresentations are pathological. All harmful non-veridical perceptions and harmful false beliefs are pathological. But this creates too many pathological mental states. Obviously it is not the case that all harmful misrepresentations are pathological. I might falsely believe that I am not as smart as my colleagues, and this false belief might have a negative impact on my well-being (e.g., a loss of self-esteem, psychological distress, or amnesia). But I might not be mentally disordered even in that case.

There are some possible responses to this objection. First, I might simply reject teleosemantics. This option, however, misses the point. As we will see, what is really needed to respond to the objection is not to deny teleosemantics but to accurately understand it. Second, I might argue that non-pathological harmful misrepresentations are not harmful enough. For example, the non-delusional false belief that I am not as smart as my colleagues is not a counterexample to my claim because it is not harmful enough. Defenders of this option would be committed to the view that the only difference between delusions and non-delusional false beliefs lies in the harmfulness condition of HDA. They are equivalent in terms of the malfunction condition; they are both malfunctional. But they are not equivalent in terms of the harmfulness condition; delusions are harmful enough to be pathological, but non-delusional false beliefs are not.

This response might or might not work. However, I am not completely satisfied with this response because I do not endorse the idea that delusions and non-delusional false beliefs are different only in terms of the harmfulness condition. In my view, they are also different in the malfunction condition because teleosemantics, properly understood, does not imply that all misrepresentations involve malfunctions. There are different versions of teleosemantics, and they need different discussions. In the following, I will talk about two notable examples: Millikan's (1984, 1989) consumer-based teleosemantics and Neander's (1995, 2013) informational teleosemantics.

Consumer-based teleosemantics: The following famous example by Dretske (1986) is useful for illustrating the basic ideas of Millikan's theory:

> Some marine bacteria have internal magnets, magnetosomes, that function like compass needles, aligning themselves (and, as a result, the bacterium) parallel to the Earth's magnetic field. Since the magnetic lines incline downward (toward geomagnetic north) in the northern hemisphere, bacteria in the northern hemisphere, oriented by their internal magnetosomes, propel themselves toward geomagnetic north. Since these organisms are capable of living only in the absence of oxygen, and since movement toward geomagnetic north will take northern bacteria away from the oxygen-rich and therefore toxic surface water and toward the comparatively oxygen-free sediment at the bottom, it is not unreasonable to speculate, as Blakemore and Frankel do, that the function of this primitive sensory system is to indicate the whereabouts of benign (i.e. anaerobic) environments.
>
> (p. 63)

What does the representational state of magnetosome represent? Does it represent the magnetic north or the oxygen-free sediment? Millikan thinks that it represents the oxygen-free sediment, not the magnetic north. In her consumer-based teleosemantics, what the representational state of magnetosome represents is determined by what the representational state needs to correspond to in order for the consumer of the state to perform its function successfully in its normal way. For the consumer (which is the motor mechanism in this case) to perform successfully, the representational state needs to correspond to the oxygen-free sediment rather than the magnetic north. After all, what is crucial for the successful functioning of the motor mechanism is to lead the bacteria to the oxygen-free sediment rather than to the magnetic north.

Millikan's account, then, allows for misrepresentations without any malfunctions. Suppose that I use a bar magnet to lead bacteria upward and, consequently, the bacteria die because of the exposure to oxygen-rich surface water. In this case, the representational state of the magnetosome misrepresents without any malfunctions. The state misrepresents because, on the one hand, it represents the oxygen-free sediment and, on the other hand, it is tokened when the oxygen-rich surface water is there instead. It does not involve any malfunctions; everything is functioning properly in the bacteria. Nothing in the bacteria is broken or damaged. It is just an unlucky situation for the bacteria.

Still, as Millikan (2004) points out, there is an important sense in which the magnetosome fails to perform its function:

> Dretske is right that the magnetosome that directs that bacterium in the wrong direction because someone holds a bar magnet overhead is not broken or malfunctioning. In that sense, it is functioning perfectly properly. But it doesn't mean that it is succeeding in performing all of its functions, any more than a perfectly functional coffeemaker is performing its function when no one has put any coffee in it. Very often things fail to perform their functions, not because they are damaged, but because the conditions they are in are not their normal operating conditions.
>
> (p. 83)

The magnetosome fails to perform its functions in the same way that a coffee maker fails to perform its function (of making coffee) when coffee beans are not put in it. In the discussions so far, I have identified 'malfunction' with 'the failure to perform a function'. But, in fact, this usage of the term is not ideal because it does not distinguish two kinds of cases in which a function fails to be performed. First, there are cases in which a function fails to be performed due to an intrinsic breakdown or damage. Second, there are cases in which a function fails to be performed due to environmental misfortune. Hereafter, I will use the term 'malfunction' for the first type of failure, and 'misfunction' for the second. The coffee maker does not malfunction but misfunctions when coffee beans are not put in it. The magnetosome does not malfunction but misfunctions when it is fooled by my bar magnet.

What is crucial for our discussion is this: it might be the case that all misrepresentations involve some misfunctions in Millikan's version of teleosemantics, but it is not the case that all misrepresentations involve malfunctions.

Informational teleosemantics: Unlike Millikan, Neander seems be committed to the idea that all misrepresentations involve malfunctions. She discusses the example of a frog (*Rana pipiens*) that catches and eats flies. The frog, however, responds not just to flies, but also to other small, dark, moving things that are not flies, such as BB bullets. Let us call the frog's representation of its target 'R'. What does R represent? Does it represent a fly or a small, dark, moving thing? (This is analogous to the question above as to whether the representational state of magnetosome represents the oxygen-free sediment or the magnetic north.) Neander thinks that R represents a small, dark, moving thing rather than a fly. This means that R does not misrepresent as long as it is caused by small, dark, moving things. It does not misrepresent, for instance, when it is caused by a BB bullet. So, when does R misrepresent? R misrepresents, according to Neander, when it is caused by something that is not a small, dark, moving thing. It misrepresents, for example, when it is caused by a snail. But this seems to imply that misrepresentation always involves some malfunctions, because there should be some malfunctions if R is caused by a snail. Neander (1995) says:

> A sick frog might R-token at a snail if it was dysfunctional in the right way. Damaging the frog's neurology, interfering in its embryological development, tinkering with its genes, giving it a virus, all of these could introduce malfunction and error.
>
> (p. 109)

But this is too quick. She also insists that the claim that misrepresentations always involve malfunctions is true, when applied to humans, only for primitive representations in the early stages of visual processing:

> Consider the case where we see a skinny cow in the dim distance and mistakenly represent it as a horse (Fodor's example). Here, we may suppose, we misrepresent without malfunctioning, and clearly the content of our perceptual representation goes beyond the physical parameters of the environmental features measured. But this sophisticated representation occurs after much visual processing has already taken place, at least, this is so on computational theories of vision. In such theories, early visual processing does not represent the cow as a horse (or as a cow) but as something which looks a certain way – as having a certain outline texture, color and so on. That is, according to conventional computational theories of perception, initially there is a representation of the physical parameters of the environment as measured by the visual system. It is much plausible that there is no misrepresentation without malfunction at this level.
>
> (p. 132)

In short, the claim that misrepresentations always involve malfunctions is not applicable to sophisticated representations such as beliefs or the perceptual representations in the later stages of visual processing. In other words, misrepresentations without any malfunctions are possible even in Neander's theory of teleosemantics.

In sum, neither Millikan's nor Neander's teleosemantics is committed to the view that all misrepresentations involve malfunctions. Misrepresentations might involve misfunctions in Millikan's account, but they do not always involve malfunctions. In Neander's theory, misrepresentations involve malfunctions in the early stages of visual processing, but it does not generalize to other kinds of misrepresentations.

3.5 Summary

I have argued that delusions are pathological because they are harmful and malfunctional. They have significant negative impacts on well-being. And, some psychological mechanisms that are directly or indirectly related to delusions fail to perform their functions due to intrinsic problems.

In this chapter, first I discussed some possible explanations of the pathology of delusional beliefs. The explanations are not fully satisfactory primarily because they are detached from the considerations about what, in general, makes a condition pathological.[22] In contrast, my account is an application of a general account of disorders by Wakefield, which explains various kinds of physical and mental disorders. Two types of objections were critically examined: (1) it is not the case that all delusions are malfunctional; and (2) being malfunctional is not sufficient for a belief to be pathological. The first type of objection came from the idea that delusions are performing psychological defense functions, that they are doxastic shear pins, and that they are produced by error management theoretic biases. In response, I argued that those ideas do not rule out the possibility that delusions involve some malfunctions. The second type of objection came from the worry that all misrepresentations involve some malfunctions according to teleosemantics. In response, I showed that notable versions of teleosemantics are, understood properly, not committed to the view that all misrepresentations involve malfunctions.

Notes

1 More precisely, the discontinuity has something to do with the failure of performing the functions and the harmfulness of the failure.
2 See also Bayne (2016).
3 See also Clutton and Gadsby (2017) and Sakakibara (2016).
4 But see Langdon and Bayne (2010). They argue that some confabulations (spontaneous ones) are delusions and that other confabulations (provoked ones) are not beliefs.
5 I am talking about the strangeness of content here. We might also talk about the strangeness of the processes. Anna's belief is not strange in the sense that it is formed in a normal belief formation process in response to some (misleading)

evidence, while DS's delusion is strange in the sense that it is not formed in a normal process. This kind of strangeness might have something to do with epistemic irrationality, which I will discuss below.

6 Here, I am talking about epistemic irrationality. See Bortolotti (2009) for a discussion of other sorts of irrationality that can be attributed to delusional beliefs.

7 However, one might expect that the bias is much stronger in people with delusions than non-clinical people. Interestingly, Corcoran and colleagues (2006) found that this prediction is false; the bias is actually stronger in non-clinical people than in people with delusions. As Corcoran and colleagues note, this result is consistent with the well-known study of the 'jumping-to-conclusions bias' (Huq, Garety, & Hemsley, 1988), which I will describe in Chapter 4. It was found in the study that people with delusions require less evidence before coming to a conclusion than people in control groups (non-clinical people and non-delusional people with schizophrenia). But, in fact, people with delusions are more rational, from a Bayesian point of view, than people in control groups: 'It may be argued that the deluded sample reached a decision at an objectively "rational" point. It may further be argued that the two control groups were somewhat over-cautious' (Huq et al., 1988, p. 809). But see also van der Leer, Hartig, Goldmanis, and McKay (2015) for an alternative understanding of the jumping-to-conclusions bias.

8 Murphy offers a broader conception of folk theory of mind that includes not just folk psychology in the narrow sense, but also 'a much richer body of beliefs and expectations about the role of hot cognition and personal interests in fixing belief' as well as 'the role of culture in shaping people's assumptions about what counts as legitimate evidence' (Murphy, 2012, p. 22). Does this broad notion of folk theory of mind help the current proposal? Probably not. Murphy argues that a belief is regarded as delusional when we are not able to provide the explanation of the belief in terms of the broad folk theory. I do not evaluate this proposal here, but it should be noted that the broad conception of folk theory is supposed to explain the delusionality of beliefs, rather than the pathology of them. And, given the difference between delusionality and pathology, it is impossible to explain both at the same time. As long as Murphy's account is successful in explaining the delusionality of beliefs, it fails in explaining the pathology of them.

9 See Bortolotti and Mameli (2012) for a similar claim.

10 Indeed, Gendler (2012) seems to think that what she proposes is an extension of folk psychology: 'The main point is simply that in developing a relatively coarse-grained folk psychology – one that makes use of the notions of belief and desire to explain intentional behaviors, and of the notion of reflex to explain behaviors that consistently occur in response to stimuli in the absence of representational mediation – it is crucial to have an intermediate category. My contention is that it should be one with the properties that I have attributed to the notion that I call alief' (pp. 799–800).

11 See also Bortolotti, Broome, and Mameli (2014) and Broome, Bortolotti, and Mameli (2010).

12 This is, strictly speaking, false – or at least misleading. I will come back to this in 3.4.2.

13 But, I admit that if a harmful malfunction is sufficient but not necessary, my proposal fails to be the fundamental explanation of the pathological nature of delusions; it is not the case that delusions are pathological in virtue of the fact that they involve harmful malfunctions.

14 See also Griffiths and Matthewson (2016) for a defense of the etiological account of disorders.

15 I thank an anonymous referee for pointing this out.

16 But I do not rule out the possibility that the harmful aspect of delusions is captured by some sophisticated versions of hedonism (e.g., Feldman, 2004).

17 Strictly speaking, the hypothesis posits malfunctioning 'connections' rather than malfunctioning 'systems' or 'mechanisms'. I assume that we can talk about proper functioning or malfunctioning of both mechanisms/systems and the connections between them. The assumption would be reasonable because, after all, natural selection designed both individual mechanisms/systems and the connections between them. Connected systems, such as the autonomic nervous system, also behave abnormally due to the disconnection from other systems, but these abnormal behaviors are, strictly speaking, not malfunctions but what I will call 'misfunctions'.

18 Another possibility is that C_B (i.e., the mechanism that initiates behavioral processes in response to beliefs and relevant motivational states) is malfunctioning. See 2.4.3.

19 See also Fineberg and Corlett (2016).

20 Another objection might come from the general skepticism about the adaptationist account of psychological mechanisms. According to this objection, delusions do not involve any malfunctions because delusion-related mechanisms (and other psychological mechanisms) do not have any functions in the evolutionary sense because the mechanisms are not the product of natural selection. Perhaps they are functionless by-products (e.g., Gould, 1991; Murphy & Woolfolk, 2000). See, e.g., Buller (2005) and Wakefield (2000).

21 Neander (1995) writes: 'The basic idea behind teleological theories of content is that this normative notion – and its distinction between proper functioning and malfunctioning – might somehow underwrite the normative notion of content – and its distinction between representation and misrepresentation' (p. 112). Again Godfrey-Smith (2006) writes: 'Much of the original appeal of teleosemantics was its ability to employ teleo-functional notions of purpose in order to deal with apparently normative aspects of semantic phenomena. In particular, the biological notion of failure to perform a proper function was used to attack the problem of misrepresentation, which had caused a lot of trouble for information-based theories' (p. 62).

22 However, I agree with Sakakibara's (2016) suggestion that the features that are mentioned in the explanations (such as strangeness or irrationality) can be reliable signs or indicators of underlying malfunctions in some cases.

References

Bayne, T. (2016). Delusion and the norms of rationality. In T. Hung & T. J. Lane (Eds.), *Rationality: Constraints and contexts* (pp. 77–94). Cambridge, MA: Academic Press.

Bortolotti, L. (2009). *Delusions and other irrational beliefs*. New York, NY: Oxford University Press.

Bortolotti, L. (2012). In defence of modest doxasticism about delusions. *Neuroethics*, 5(1), 39–53.

Bortolotti, L. (2015). *Irrationality*. Cambridge: Polity Press.

Bortolotti, L., Broome, M. R., & Mameli, M. (2014). Delusions and responsibility for action: Insights from the Breivik case. *Neuroethics*, *7*(3), 377–382.

Bortolotti, L., Gunn, R., & Sullivan-Bissett, E. (2016). What makes a belief delusional? In I. McCarthy, K. Sellevold, & O. Smith (Eds.), *Cognitive confusions: Dreams, delusions and illusions in early modern culture* (pp. 37–51). Cambridge: Legenda.

Bortolotti, L., & Mameli, M. (2012). Self-deception, delusion and the boundaries of folk psychology. *Humana.Mente*, *20*, 203–221.

Broome, M. R., Bortolotti, L., & Mameli, M. (2010). Moral responsibility and mental illness: A case study. *Cambridge Quarterly of Healthcare Ethics*, *19*(2), 179–187.

Buller, D. (2005). *Adapting minds: Evolutionary psychology and the persistent quest for human nature*. Cambridge, MA: The MIT Press.

Butler, P. V. (2000). Reverse Othello syndrome subsequent to traumatic brain injury. *Psychiatry*, *63*(1), 85–92.

Clutton, P., & Gadsby, S. (2017). Delusions, harmful dysfunctions, and treatable conditions. *Neuroethics*, online first. Retrieved from https://doi.org/10.1007/s12152-017-9347-2.

Coltheart, M., Menzies, P., & Sutton, J. (2010). Abductive inference and delusional belief. *Cognitive Neuropsychiatry*, *15*(1–3), 261–287.

Connors, M. H., Barnier, A. J., Coltheart, M., Cox, R. E., & Langdon, R. (2012). Mirrored-self misidentification in the hypnosis laboratory: Recreating the delusion from its component factors. *Cognitive Neuropsychiatry*, *17*(2), 151–176.

Corcoran, R., Cummins, S., Rowse, G., Moore, R., Blackwood, N., Howard, R., . . . & Bentall, R. P. (2006). Reasoning under uncertainty: Heuristic judgments in patients with persecutory delusions or depression. *Psychological Medicine*, *36*(8), 1109–1118.

Dretske, F. (1986). Misrepresentation. In R. Bogdan (Ed.), *Belief: Form, content and function* (pp. 17–36). Oxford: Clarendon Press.

Easton, J. A., Schipper, L. D., & Shackelford, T. K. (2006). Why the adaptationist perspective must be considered: The example of morbid jealousy. *Behavioral and Brain Sciences*, *29*(4), 411–412.

Easton, J. A., Schipper, L. D., & Shackelford, T. K. (2007). Morbid jealousy from an evolutionary psychological perspective. *Evolution and Human Behavior*, *28*(6), 399–402.

Egan, A. (2009). Imagination, delusion, and self-deception. In T. Bayne & J. Fernández (Eds.), *Delusions and self-deception: Motivational and affective influences on belief formation* (pp. 263–280). Hove: Psychology Press.

Ellis, H. D., & Young, A. W. (1990). Accounting for delusional misidentifications. *The British Journal of Psychiatry*, *157*(2), 239–248.

Feldman, F. (2004). *Pleasure and the good life: Concerning the nature, varieties and plausibility of hedonism*. Oxford: Clarendon Press.

Fineberg, S. K., & Corlett, P. R. (2016). The doxastic shear pin: Delusions as errors of learning and memory. *Cognitive Neuropsychiatry*, *21*(1), 73–89.

Freeman, D. (2006). Delusions in the nonclinical population. *Current Psychiatry Reports*, *8*(3), 191–204.

Friedrich, J. (1993). Primary Error Detection and Minimization (PEDMIN) strategies in social cognition: A reinterpretation of confirmation bias phenomena. *Psychological Review*, *100*(2), 298.

Gendler, T. S. (2008). Alief and belief. *The Journal of Philosophy, 105*(10), 634–663.

Gendler, T. S. (2012). Between reason and reflex: Response to commentators. *Analysis, 72*(4), 799–811.

Godfrey-Smith, P. (2006). Mental representation, naturalism, and teleosemantics. In G. MacDonald & D. Papineau (Eds.), *Teleosemantics: New philosophical essays* (pp. 42–68). Oxford: Clarendon Press.

Gould, S. J. (1991). Exaptation: A crucial tool for an evolutionary psychology. *Journal of Social Issues, 47*(3), 43–65.

Griffiths, P. E., & Matthewson, J. (2016). Evolution, dysfunction, and disease: A reappraisal. *The British Journal for the Philosophy of Science, 69*(2), 301–327.

Haselton, M. G., & Buss, D. M. (2000). Error management theory: A new perspective on biases in cross-sex mind reading. *Journal of Personality and Social Psychology, 78*(1), 81.

Huq, S. F., Garety, P. A., & Hemsley, D. R. (1988). Probabilistic judgements in deluded and non-deluded subjects. *The Quarterly Journal of Experimental Psychology, 40*(4), 801–812.

Kahneman, D., & Tversky, A. (1973). On the psychology of prediction. *Psychological Review, 80*(4), 237.

Kapur, S. (2003). Psychosis as a state of aberrant salience: A framework linking biology, phenomenology, and pharmacology in schizophrenia. *American Journal of Psychiatry, 160*(1), 13–23.

Langdon, R., & Bayne, T. (2010). Delusion and confabulation: Mistakes of perceiving, remembering and believing. *Cognitive Neuropsychiatry, 15*(1–3), 319–345.

Maher, B. A. (1974). Delusional thinking and perceptual disorder. *Journal of Individual Psychology, 30*(1), 98–113.

McKay, R. (2012). Delusional inference. *Mind & Language, 27*(3), 330–355.

McKay, R., & Dennett, D. (2009). The evolution of misbelief. *Behavioral and Brain Sciences, 32*(6), 493–510.

McKay, R., Langdon, R., & Coltheart, M. (2005). "Sleights of mind": Delusions, defences, and self-deception. *Cognitive Neuropsychiatry, 10*(4), 305–326.

Mele, A. R. (1999). Twisted self-deception. *Philosophical Psychology, 12*(2), 117–137.

Millikan, R. G. (1984). *Language, thought, and other biological categories: New foundations for realism.* Cambridge, MA: The MIT Press.

Millikan, R. G. (1989). Biosemantics. *Journal of Philosophy,* 86, 281–297.

Millikan, R. G. (2004). *Varieties of meaning: The 2002 Jean Nicod lectures.* Cambridge, MA: The MIT Press.

Mishara, A. L., & Corlett, P. (2009). Are delusions biologically adaptive? Salvaging the doxastic shear pin. *Behavioral and Brain Sciences, 32*(6), 530–531.

Murphy, D. (2012). The folk epistemology of delusions. *Neuroethics, 5*(1), 19–22.

Murphy, D. (2013). Delusions, modernist epistemology and irrational belief. *Mind & Language, 28*(1), 113–124.

Murphy, D., & Woolfolk, R. L. (2000). The harmful dysfunction analysis of mental disorder. *Philosophy, Psychiatry, & Psychology, 7*(4), 241–252.

Neander, K. (1995). Misrepresenting & malfunctioning. *Philosophical Studies, 79*(2), 109–141.

Neander, K. (2013). Toward an informational teleosemantics. In D. Ryder, J. Kingsbury, & K. Williford (Eds.), *Millikan and her critics* (pp. 21–36). Chichester: Wiley-Blackwell.

Nesse, R. (1998). Emotional disorders in evolutionary perspective. *Psychology and Psychotherapy: Theory, Research and Practice, 71*(4), 397–415.

Nozick, R. (1974). *Anarchy, state and utopia*. Oxford: Basil Blackwell.

Perilloux, C., Easton, J. A., & Buss, D. M. (2012). The misperception of sexual interest. *Psychological Science, 23*(2), 146–151.

Reimer, M. (2010a). Only a philosopher or a madman: Impractical delusions in philosophy and psychiatry. *Philosophy, Psychiatry, & Psychology, 17*(4), 315–328.

Reimer, M. (2010b). Distinguishing between the psychiatrically and philosophically deluded: Easier said than done. *Philosophy, Psychiatry, & Psychology, 17*(4), 341–346.

Sakakibara, E. (2016). Irrationality and pathology of beliefs. *Neuroethics, 9*(2), 147–157.

Stone, T., & Young, A. W. (1997). Delusions and brain injury: The philosophy and psychology of belief. *Mind & Language, 12*(3–4), 327–364.

Sullivan-Bissett, E., Bortolotti, L., Broome, M., & Mameli, M. (2016). Moral and legal implications of the continuity between delusional and nondelusional beliefs. In K. Geert, L. Keuck, & R. Hauswald (Eds.), *Vagueness in psychiatry* (pp. 191–210). Oxford: Oxford University Press.

Tengland, P. (2001). *Mental health: A philosophical analysis*. Dordrecht: Kluwer.

van der Leer, L., Hartig, B., Goldmanis, M., & McKay, R. (2015). Delusion proneness and "jumping to conclusions": Relative and absolute effects. *Psychological Medicine, 45*(6), 1253–1262.

Wakefield, J. C. (1992a). The concept of mental disorder: On the boundary between biological facts and social values. *American Psychologist, 47*(3), 373–388.

Wakefield, J. C. (1992b). Disorder as harmful dysfunction: A conceptual critique of DSM-III-R's definition of mental disorder. *Psychological Review, 99*(2), 232–247.

Wakefield, J. C. (2000). Spandrels, vestigial organs, and such: Reply to Murphy and Woolfolk's "The Harmful Dysfunction Analysis of Mental Disorder". *Philosophy, Psychiatry, & Psychology, 7*(4), 253–269.

Wakefield, J. C. (2011). Darwin, functional explanation, and the philosophy of psychiatry. In P. R. Adriaens & A. De Block (Eds.), *Maladapting minds: Philosophy, psychiatry, and evolutionary theory* (pp. 43–172). New York, NY: Oxford University Press.

4 Etiology

4.1 Overview

My discussions so far support the malfunctional belief hypothesis, according to which delusions are malfunctional beliefs. This hypothesis has two major sub-hypotheses: (1) delusions are beliefs, and (2) delusions are malfunctional. Sub-hypothesis 1 was defended in Chapter 2; delusions are produced and consumed by the cognitive mechanisms with the right kind of functions in an attempt to perform the right kind of functions (the doxastic mechanism hypothesis 2). Sub-hypothesis 2 was defended in Chapter 3; some of these cognitive mechanisms (and other mechanisms that are indirectly relevant) are malfunctioning or, in other words, failing to perform their functions due to intrinsic problems (the malfunction thesis). In defending these sub-hypotheses, I made some assumptions (in particular, empiricist assumptions) about the process of delusion formation. The aim of this chapter is to make these assumptions explicit and articulate my commitments to the process of delusion formation. This is, in effect, to answer the etiology question.

It is important to note that it is impossible to solve all the mysteries about delusion formation in this chapter. Delusion formation is an open empirical issue, and a complete understanding of the process requires much more empirical data and clinical observations than we currently have. My aim in this chapter is modest: I only try to show that an empiricist theory is at least on the right track. The theory I will be defending is a version of two-factor empiricism. I will describe the central ideas of the two-factor theory and provide an inference-to-the-best explanation argument for the theory (**4.2**). I will then discuss the nature of the second factor and defend a particular hypothesis according to which the second factor is the bias towards observational adequacy (**4.3**). After, I will discuss the relationship between the two-factor theory and the prediction-error theory, which will lead me to propose a way of incorporating the prediction-error theoretic ideas into the two-factor framework (**4.4**).[1]

Here are some notes on my terminology in this chapter:

'The two-factor theory': The central figure in the two-factor theory camp is Max Coltheart. All the central ideas of the theory come from the papers by Coltheart and his colleagues. But I avoid the *ad hominem* terminology according to which 'the two-factor theory' simply means 'Coltheart's theory'. A reason is that Coltheart's view has been evolving from his early papers to recent ones. For example, a remarkable recent development is about his account of the nature of the second factor (Coltheart et al., 2010). Another, more important reason is that it is theoretically more useful to abstract away some of the details associated with a particular individual (i.e., Coltheart) and consider the general theoretical framework. What I take to be the general two-factor framework is characterized by some central ideas. (I will say more about what the central ideas are in 4.2.1.) And, within this framework, there are different versions of the two-factor theory with different details. Thus, in my terminology, an account of the process of delusion formation is a version of the two-factor theory if it shares the central ideas. It is not necessary to share all of Coltheart's commitments about the details, such as the view that the first factor of the Capgras delusion is not consciously accessible (Coltheart et al., 2010) or the view that the second factor has something to do with the right hemisphere abnormalities (Coltheart, 2007). For instance, the influential account of the Capgras delusion (and other delusions of misidentification) by Stone and Young (1997) share what I take to be the central ideas of the two-factor theory, and hence it is regarded as a version of the two-factor theory.[2]

'Delusion formation': It is often said that the two-factor theory is a theory of 'delusion formation'. This terminology, however, could give us the false impression that the two-factor theory only aims to explain the process in which delusional hypotheses are adopted in a person's belief system. The two-factor theory aims to explain not only the process in which delusional hypotheses are adopted but also the process in which, after they are adopted, they are maintained despite counterevidence. A remarkable feature of delusions is that they are firmly maintained 'despite what constitutes incontrovertible and obvious proof or evidence to the contrary' (American Psychiatric Association, 2013, p. 819), and explaining this feature is one of the aims of the two-factor theory. In this book, I use the term 'formation' in a broad sense, referring to the composite causal process consisting of the adoption process and the maintenance process. When I say that a delusion is 'formed', therefore, I mean that a delusional

hypothesis is adopted and maintained. When I say that a delusion is 'not formed', I mean that it is not the case that the delusional hypothesis is adopted and maintained; either the hypothesis is not adopted in the first place, or it is adopted but not maintained.

'Belief': Two notions of 'belief' are present in recent discussions of the delusion formation process: outright belief and graded belief (or credence). The prediction-error theory is often expressed within the Bayesian probabilistic framework where the notion of 'belief' is the graded one. In contrast, the notion of 'belief' in the two-factor theory tends to be the outright one (although recent Bayesian versions of the two-factor theory incorporate the graded notion). One might think that an outright belief reduces to a graded belief, in which case the latter is more fundamental than the former. For example, an outright belief just is a graded belief above a certain threshold. Alternatively, one might argue that a graded belief reduces to an outright belief, in which case the latter is more fundamental than the former. For example, a graded belief just is an outright belief with probabilistic propositional content, such as the outright belief that there is a 50% chance that it will snow tomorrow. Although I acknowledge the philosophical import of these issues (e.g., Leitgeb, 2017), I will not discuss them further here. I simply assume that outright beliefs and graded beliefs are not distinct states. This assumption enables us to compare the prediction-error theory, in which a delusion is typically regarded as a graded belief, and the two-factor theory, in which a delusion is typically regarded as an outright belief, as two theories to explain the same phenomenon.

4.2   The two-factor theory

4.2.1   Basic ideas

The two-factor theory primarily aims to explain the delusions that can be monothematic (i.e., concerning a single theme) and neuropsychological (i.e., caused by neuropsychological deficits). The two-factor theory is a form of empiricism according to which delusions are formed in response to abnormal data, but it has an additional commitment that the data do not explain everything about delusion formation.

Let us consider the Capgras delusion as an example. According to the standard account (e.g., Ellis & Young, 1990; Stone & Young, 1997), the Capgras delusion is formed in response to the abnormal data generated by abnormal autonomic activities. The two-factor theorists, however, insist that the abnormal data are not sufficient for the formation of the Capgras delusion. The abnormal data are a factor, 'the first factor', but there should be another factor, 'the second factor', to complete the explanation. Broadly speaking, there are two possible versions of the two-factor theory corresponding to two possible hypotheses on the role of the second factor. First, the first factor is not sufficient for the adoption (and the maintenance) of the Capgras delusion. In this case, the role of the second factor is to explain the adoption (and the maintenance) of the delusion (e.g., McKay, 2012; Stone & Young, 1997). I call this 'the adoption two-factor theory'. Second, the first factor is sufficient for the adoption, but not for the maintenance, of the Capgras delusion. In this case, the role of the second factor is to explain the maintenance of the Capgras delusion (e.g., Coltheart et al., 2010). I call this 'the maintenance two-factor theory'.

The two-factor theory thus posits two explanatory factors in the process of delusion formation, which play different explanatory roles. In particular, the first factor explains the theme of the delusion.[3] In other words, the first factor explains why a delusion has a particular delusional theme. The abnormal data generated by reduced autonomic activities, for example, explain why the Capgras delusion has its particular theme (i.e., a familiar individual being replaced by an imposter). The second factor, on the other hand, explains the formation of the delusion.[4] More precisely, the second factor in the adoption two-factor theory explains why the delusion is adopted in the belief system (and maintained despite counterevidence), while the second factor in the maintenance two-factor theory explains why the delusion is maintained despite counterevidence. I will say more about the second factor in the next section.

There are some popular assumptions about the first and the second factors. First, different kinds of delusions have different first factors. This claim follows from the idea that the first factor is responsible for the theme of a delusion together with the observation that different kinds of delusions have different themes. Second, the second factor is often regarded as being the same in most, if not all, kinds of delusions. This follows from the idea that the second factor is responsible for the formation of a delusion, together with the observation that most, if not all, kinds of delusions are formed in similar processes. Third, the second factor is often regarded as having something to do with abnormalities in the right hemisphere of the brain. This view comes from the observation that people with monothematic and neuropsychological delusions tend to have right hemisphere deficits.

But perhaps these assumptions should not be taken too seriously. For example, as Young, Leafhead, and Szulecka (1994) suggest, people with the Cotard delusion (i.e., the delusion that one is dead or disembodied) might have the same kind of abnormal data as people with the Capgras delusion; they explain the data in different ways.[5] This suggestion goes against the first assumption (and probably the second assumption, i.e., different explanations correspond to different second factors). Again, Coltheart, Langdon, and McKay (2011) discuss the idea that the second factor of the alien abduction delusion (i.e., the delusion that one was abducted by aliens) is the predisposition to accept 'New Age' beliefs, which goes against the second assumption (because this second factor is not shared by other delusions) and the third assumption (because this second factor has nothing to do with the right hemisphere abnormalities). Thus, it is safe not to take those assumptions to be indispensable for the two-factor theory.

The two-factor theory is often contrasted with Maher-style theory (e.g., Maher, 1974; see also Gerrans, 2002; Reimer, 2009), which is sometimes called 'the one-factor theory'. Maher is often associated with the view that a delusion is formed as a reasonable response to abnormal data ('the reasonableness thesis' hereafter). Indeed, he argues the process in which a person adopts a delusional hypothesis is indistinguishable from the process in which a scientist adopts a scientific hypothesis. It is often said that the two-factor theory denies the reasonableness thesis and that is why the two-factor theory contradicts Maher-style theory. However, the relationship between the two-factor theory and Maher-style theory is complicated because one can endorse the reasonableness thesis without abandoning the two-factor theory. The maintenance two-factor theorists can hold such a view. Perhaps adopting a delusional hypothesis is a reasonable thing to do, which is consistent with the reasonableness thesis. But maintaining the hypothesis despite counterevidence is not reasonable, which is why the second factor is needed to explain the maintenance process (e.g., Coltheart et al., 2010). Even the adoption two-factor theorists can endorse the reasonableness thesis, at least in principle. For example, they can maintain that adopting a delusional hypothesis is reasonable, but still the second factor is involved in the adoption process. Perhaps the second factor consists in the abnormal degree of reasonableness; people with delusions are much more reasonable in responding to data than non-clinical people. This hypothesis might be coherent with some empirical studies (e.g., Corcoran et al., 2006; Huq, Garety, & Hemsley, 1988).[6]

4.2.2   An inference-to-the-best-explanation argument

Having clarified the central ideas of the two-factor theory, I will now discuss the arguments for the theory. I first assume that empiricism is on the right track. In other words, I assume that delusions are formed in response to abnormal data.[7] The fundamental commitment of the two-factor theory, which distinguishes it from other empiricist theories, is that abnormal data are not explanatorily sufficient. Another factor is needed for a complete account of the process of delusion formation. What are the arguments for this commitment?

There are several arguments that are implicit or explicit in previous papers by the two-factor theorists. My aim in this chapter is not to add another argument but rather to provide a new interpretation of existing arguments. The existing arguments refer to some observations that are in favor of the two-factor theory. My view is that the observations should not be considered independently or separately from each other. Rather, they should be considered jointly in the form of a single inference-to-the-best explanation argument. In other words, the best explanation of the relevant observations is provided by the two-factor theoretic hypothesis that the second factor is necessary. Independently, none of the observations are conclusive; they are open to alternative interpretations. Jointly, however, they strongly support the two-factor theory in the form of an inference-to-the-best-explanation argument. This is a common feature of inference-to-the-best-explanation arguments in general. For example, the footprint at a crime scene might not be conclusive evidence for a hypothesis about the perpetuator; it might be open to alternative interpretations. Jointly, together with other evidence, however, it might strongly support the hypothesis in the form of an inference-to-the-best-explanation argument.

Alternative explanations: The delusional hypothesis is not the only available hypothesis that accounts for abnormal data. There are many other alternative hypotheses, including the ones that might be better explanations of the data. The first factor does not explain why the delusional hypothesis, rather than alternative ones, is favored. For instance, Stone and Young (1997) point out that the abnormal data generated by reduced autonomic activities are not enough to explain why the Capgras hypothesis, and not another hypothesis, is favored:

> Why does the patient form such a bizarre belief to explain their anomalous experience and not adopt what Maher calls 'the more natural explanation' by simply saying that things seem strange and stopping there? [. . .] this is exactly what many people with brain injuries actually do, and they are therefore not considered deluded. The difference in Capgras cases seems to be that they adopt what is to others a much more implausible account of what has happened. This willingness on the part of people experiencing the Capgras delusion to offer such an extraordinary and bizarre account needs to be explained. [. . .] The perceptual deficit account is clearly incomplete.
>
> (p. 341)

Note that this observation about alternative hypotheses can be interpreted in at least two ways, corresponding to the adoption/maintenance distinction.

Stone and Young offer the adoption theoretic interpretation, according to which the abnormal data are not enough to explain the fact that the Capgras hypothesis, rather than another hypothesis, is adopted. According to this interpretation, the role of the second factor is to explain why the Capgras hypothesis is adopted (and maintained). In contrast, according to the maintenance theoretic interpretation (e.g., Coltheart et al., 2010), the abnormal data explain the fact that the Capgras hypothesis is adopted, but not the fact that the hypothesis is maintained despite the counterevidence available at the post-adoption stage.

Dissociation: The second observation is that the first factors and delusions are dissociable from one another; in particular, one can have the first factor without forming the relevant delusion. For example, just like people with the Capgras delusion, people with damage to the ventromedial prefrontal cortex (vmPFC) exhibit reduced autonomic activities in response to familiar faces (Tranel, Damasio, & Damasio, 1995). This suggests that people with vmPFC damage are also faced with the data generated by reduced autonomic activities. However, people with vmPFC damage do not typically form the Capgras delusion, which seems to show that one can have the abnormal data generated by reduced autonomic activities without forming the Capgras delusion. But, then, either the abnormal data are not causally responsible for the Capgras delusion at all, or, in addition to the abnormal data, there is another factor that explains why people with the Capgras delusion, but not people with vmPFC damage, form the delusion. The first option is unlikely because the theme of the Capgras delusion has an obvious connection to the abnormal data. Therefore, the second hypothesis, the two-factor theoretic one, seems to be the most plausible option.

I have said that people with vmPFC damage typically do not 'form' the Capgras delusion. This can be interpreted in two different ways, corresponding to the adoption/maintenance distinction. According to the adoption theoretic interpretation, a person with vmPFC damage does not adopt the Capgras hypothesis in the first place. What the vmPFC cases show is that one can have the abnormal data without adopting the Capgras hypothesis. In this case, the second factor is needed to explain the adoption (and the maintenance) of the Capgras hypothesis (e.g., McKay, 2012; Stone & Young, 1997). In contrast, according to the maintenance theoretic interpretation, a person with vmPFC damage adopts the Capgras hypothesis once but does not maintain it in the face of the counterevidence available at the post-adoption stage. What the vmPFC cases show is that one can have the abnormal data without maintaining the Capgras hypothesis. In this case, the second factor is needed to explain the maintenance, rather than the adoption, of the Capgras hypothesis (e.g., Coltheart et al., 2010).

Similar arguments can be made with respect to a wide range of delusions that can be monothematic and neuropsychological (e.g., Coltheart, 2007; Coltheart et al., 2011; Davies, Coltheart, Langdon, & Breen, 2001). For example, people with the Cotard delusion and people with schizophrenia who experience global affective flattening might share the same (or similar) abnormal data, but the latter typically do not form the delusion. People with the delusion of alien control (i.e., the delusion that one's own behavior is controlled by external forces) and people with depersonalization disorder might share the same (or similar) abnormal data, but the latter typically do not form the delusion.

Neuropsychological abnormalities: The third observation is about the presence of neuropsychological impairments. For instance, individuals with monothematic and neuropsychological delusions can have deficits in the right hemisphere of the brain, in particular, the right prefrontal cortex (rPFC) (e.g., Coltheart, 2007).[8] Such neuropsychological abnormalities might be the neural basis of the second factor. This argument does not seem to be directly applicable to delusions without neuropsychological impairments. However, Coltheart (2010) suggests that it might be indirectly applicable to them because 'the distinction between neuropsychological and non-neuropsychological delusions (sometimes referred to as the distinction between organic and functional psychosis) is not at all clear-cut' (p. 25).

Cognitive biases: The fourth observation is about the presence of cognitive abnormalities or biases that are apparently independent of the first factor. The most famous finding is about the jumping-to-conclusions bias, which is the bias of coming to a conclusion more quickly than non-clinical subjects. In a well-known study (Huq et al., 1988), participants observed the beads drawn from a jar and determined which of the following hypotheses is true; (1) the jar contains 85 pink beads and 15 green beads, or (2) it contains 15 pink beads and 85 green beads. Huq and colleagues found that participants in the delusion group tended to 'jump to the conclusion'; they required less evidence (i.e., fewer beads drawn from the jar) before coming to a conclusion than the participants in the non-clinical group.[9]

Another bias that might be causally relevant is the bias against disconfirmatory evidence (Moritz & Woodward, 2006; Woodward, Moritz, Cuttler, & Whitman, 2006), which is the bias of failing to incorporate the evidence that is against one's prior belief.[10] The role of the cognitive biases such as the jumping-to-conclusions bias or the bias against disconfirmatory evidence is not well understood,[11] but it is likely that some of those biases are causally relevant in the delusion formation process.

Individually, none of the observations above are conclusive; they might be open to different interpretations. For instance, some authors offer another interpretation of vmPFC damage, according to which people with vmPFC damage do not form the Capgras delusion, not because they lack the second factor but because they do not share the same abnormal data with people with the Capgras delusion (e.g., Hohwy & Rosenberg, 2005; Reimer, 2009). Nonetheless, when considering the observations jointly, the most plausible explanation seems to be the two-factor theoretic explanation; the first factor is not causally sufficient, and we need to posit another factor. Non-two-factor theoretic explanations of the observations are also available, but it is likely that they are more *ad hoc* and/or theoretically complicated than the two-factor theoretic one. For instance, those who offer the alternative interpretation of vmPFC damage, according to which people with vmPFC damage do not share the same abnormal data with people with the Capgras delusion, need to explain other observations, such as neuropsychological abnormalities or cognitive biases. Perhaps they tell different stories to explain (or explain away) different observations, in which case their overall account is *ad hoc* and/or complicated. The two-factor theorists, on the other hand, tell a simple and unified story of all of the relevant observations.

4.3   Second factor and Bayesian approaches

The inference-to-the-best-explanation argument above shows that the second factor is present in the process of delusion formation, but it does not say what the factor is exactly. The argument itself is consistent with different hypotheses about the nature of the second factor.

All two-factor theorists agree on the presence of the second factor, but they have different views on the nature of it. In an early paper by Davies and colleagues (2001), for example, the second factor is vaguely characterized as 'the loss of the ability to reject a candidate for belief on the grounds of its implausibility and its inconsistency with everything else that the patient knows' (p. 154). In recent papers, the two-factor theorists adopt some ideas from the Bayesian model of belief updating and propose more informative accounts of the second factor (e.g., Coltheart et al., 2010; McKay, 2012).[12] According to Coltheart and colleagues (2010), for example, the Capgras delusion is inferentially formed in response to the abnormal data generated by reduced autonomic activities, and the inferential step is perfectly Bayesian-rational. Let us think about the case in which a person has the Capgras delusion about his wife. Let Hs be the hypothesis that the woman in front of him is a stranger, let Hw be the hypothesis that the woman in front of him is his wife, and let O be the observation of abnormal autonomic activities. The following follows from Bayes' theorem:

$$\frac{P(Hs|O)}{P(Hw|O)} = \frac{P(Hs) \times P(O|Hs)}{P(Hw) \times P(O|Hw)}$$

Coltheart and colleagues make the following suggestion:

$P(Hs) < P(Hw)$

$P(O|Hs) \gg P(O|Hw)$

$P(Hs|O) > P(Hw|O)$

In other words, Hw has a higher prior probability than Hs. But it is outweighed by the likelihood ratio, which overwhelmingly favors Hs. As the result, Hs gets a higher posterior probability than Hw. Assuming that this is the way the person actually reasons, Coltheart and colleagues argue that the Capgras delusion is adopted in a Bayesian-rational probabilistic inference.

According to Coltheart and colleagues, this inferential adoption process is perfectly rational and normal, which suggests that there is no second factor in the stage of hypothesis adoption. Rather, the second factor lies in the post-adoption stage where the person faces newly available counterevidence to Hs (such as the testimony of reliable friends and doctors). According to Coltheart and colleagues, a person with the Capgras delusion fails to incorporate the new body of evidence in the post-adoption stage, which is why he maintains the delusional hypothesis. This bias of neglecting newly available evidence is the second factor; it explains the difference between people with the Capgras delusion and people with vmPFC damage. People in both groups adopt Hs through a Bayesian-rational probabilistic inference. But, in the face of the newly available counterevidence, people with vmPFC damage give up Hs and adopt Hw instead. On the other hand, people with the Capgras delusion fail to do so because of the bias of neglecting newly available evidence. This proposal is a version of the maintenance two-factor theory; the role of the second factor is to explain the maintenance process rather than the adoption process.

This is certainly an interesting proposal, but it has some problems. In particular, if people with the Capgras delusion have the bias of neglecting new evidence, then how can we explain the fact that they do not neglect the new evidence acquired at the adoption stage, i.e., the abnormal data generated by reduced autonomic activities? According to the proposal by Coltheart and colleagues, the person in the example above adopts Hs because Hs gets a higher probability than Hw given the abnormal data. Here, he does not neglect the abnormal data. Why is it, then, that he does not neglect the new evidence at the adoption stage (i.e., the abnormal data) but does neglect the new evidence at the maintenance stage (e.g., testimony of friends and doctors)? To be consistent, Coltheart and colleagues might say that the bias of neglecting new evidence is acquired after Hs is adopted (and thus the abnormal data are not neglected) and before counterevidence to Hs becomes available (and thus the testimony of friends and doctors is neglected). But this chronological scenario is not realistic (cf. McKay, 2012).

McKay (2012) presents an alternative and more promising account of the second factor. He disagrees with the claim by Coltheart and colleagues that the Capgras delusion is adopted in a Bayesian-rational probabilistic inference. According to McKay, the sample estimation of prior probabilities by Coltheart and colleagues is unrealistic. Given a more realistic assignment of prior probabilities, *Hs* does not get a higher posterior probability than *Hw*. This means that the adoption of *Hs*, rather than *Hw*, is not Bayesian-rational.

McKay accepts Stone and Young's (1997) idea that the process of delusion formation involves the bias towards observational adequacy ('the observational adequacy bias' hereafter), i.e., the biased tendency to place more emphasis on incorporating new observations into their belief system ('observational adequacy') than keeping their existing beliefs as long as possible ('doxastic conservatism').[13]

McKay provides a probabilistic interpretation of the observational adequacy bias, according to which the observational adequacy bias is mathematically understood as the bias of discounting the prior probability ratio (the 'discounting priors bias' hereafter). Here is McKay's story about the Capgras delusion:

$$P(Hs) << P(Hw)$$

$$P(O|Hs) >> P(O|Hw)$$

$$P(Hs|O) > P(Hw|O)$$

Hw has a much higher prior probability than *Hs*, according to the realistic estimation of prior probabilities. However, the likelihood ratio overwhelmingly favors *Hs*. Due to the discounting priors bias, the prior probability ratio in favor of *Hw* is discounted, and the likelihood ratio in favor of *Hs* is overemphasized. As the result, *Hs* gets a higher posterior probability than *Hw*. According to McKay, this bias is the second factor; it explains the difference between people with the Capgras delusion and people with vmPFC damage. People with vmPFC damage, without the discounting priors bias, adopt *Hw*, whereas people with the Capgras delusion, with the discounting priors bias, adopt *Hs* instead. This is a version of the adoption two-factor theory; the role of the second factor (i.e., the discounting priors bias) is to explain the adoption (and the maintenance) of delusions.

I am inclined to agree with Stone, Young, and McKay that, for many delusions, the second factor is the observational adequacy bias or, put mathematically, the discounting priors bias. Some remarks are needed to avoid potential confusions and misunderstandings. This proposal might be associated with the assumption that, unlike people with delusions, non-clinical people tend to incorporate prior probabilities more or less Bayesian-rationally in the belief updating process. But this assumption is probably wrong. As I already noted in Chapter 3, the famous study by Kahneman and Tversky (1973) on the base-rate neglect reveals a widespread tendency to neglect the base-rate information, which is mathematically understood as the tendency to neglect prior probabilities. It is therefore safe to assume that, strictly speaking, the discounting priors bias is not peculiar to people with delusions. Perhaps people with vmPFC damage also have the bias, in which case it is difficult to maintain the claim that what distinguishes people with the Capgras delusion from people with vmPFC damage is the presence of the discounting priors bias. In order to avoid potential difficulties of this kind, I argue that what distinguishes people with the Capgras delusions from people with vmPFC damage is not the presence of the discounting priors bias itself, but rather the relative strength of the discounting priors bias; the discounting priors bias is stronger in people with the Capgras delusion than in people with vmPFC damage.[14] In this chapter, when I refer to 'the observational adequacy bias' and 'the discounting priors bias', I am talking about the relative strength of the biases rather than the presence of them.

4.4 Two-factors and prediction-errors

4.4.1 The prediction-error theory

The prediction-error theory (e.g., Adams, Stephan, Brown, Frith, & Friston, 2013; Corlett, Taylor, Wang, Fletcher, & Krystal, 2010; Corlett, Honey, & Fletcher, 2016; Fletcher & Frith, 2009; Frith & Friston, 2012) is another influential theory of delusions (in particular, delusions in the context of schizophrenia). The prediction-error theory is an application of a general theory of brain functions, which is often called 'the predictive-coding account' or 'the predictive processing account' (e.g., Clark, 2013, 2016; Friston, 2005, 2010; Hohwy, 2013).

The central idea of the prediction-error theory is that delusions are explained by some disturbances in the processing of prediction-errors (i.e., mismatches between predictions and actual outcomes). In a study by Corlett and colleagues (2007), two groups of participants – a group of people with a diagnosis of first-episode psychosis and a group of non-clinical individuals – were tested in an experiment in which they learned the associations between certain food items and a hypothetical person's allergic reactions to them and, then, made predictions about the hypothetical person's reaction to new food items. Their predictions were subsequently confirmed (correct prediction) or disconfirmed (prediction-error) by the feedback they received from the experimenter, while the activity of the rPFC (which had been identified as a reliable marker of prediction-error processing in earlier studies, including the study by Corlett and colleagues (2004)), was monitored with fMRI. In the non-clinical group, rPFC activity was much greater when predictions were disconfirmed than when they were confirmed; the brain was 'surprised' when predictions turned out to be false. On the other hand, this asymmetry in rPFC activity was missing in the psychotic group; the brain was 'surprised' not only when predictions were disconfirmed but also when they were confirmed. The study also found that the severity of this brain abnormality correlated with the severity of the delusion.[15]

If the brains of people with schizophrenia have this type of abnormality, then they might find the events they experience and the objects they encounter abnormal and surprising, even though the events and objects are completely normal and unsurprising for non-clinical individuals. Some delusions in the context of schizophrenia could be understood as hypotheses explaining such abnormal and surprising events and objects. Corlett, Krystal, Taylor, and Fletcher (2009) summarize their idea as follows:

> under the influence of inappropriate prediction-error signal, possibly as a consequence of dopamine dysregulation, events that are insignificant and merely coincident seem to demand attention, feel important and relate to each other in meaningful ways. Delusions ultimately arise as a means of explaining these odd experiences.
>
> (p. 1)

It is often said, especially by the prediction-error theorists, that the two-factor theory and the prediction-error theory are alternative accounts of the process of delusion formation. For example, Corlett and colleagues argue that 'prediction error driven Bayesian models of delusions subsume both factors into a single deficit in Bayesian inference; noise in predictive learning mechanisms engender inappropriate percepts which update future priors, leading to the formation and maintenance of delusions' (Corlett et al., 2010, p. 357). In my view, however, the two-factor theory and the prediction-error theory do not have to be regarded as incompatible alternatives. I argued elsewhere that the main arguments for the incompatibility of the two theories should be rejected (Bortolotti & Miyazono, 2015; Miyazono, Bortolotti, & Broome, 2014). Here I make a stronger claim. The two-factor theory and the prediction-error theory are not only logically compatible with each other but can also be combined in a particular way. More precisely, the basic ideas of the prediction-error theory can be incorporated into the two-factor framework to form a hybrid theory of delusion formation. I will now outline the hybrid theory (**4.4.2**) and discuss some advantages of the theory (**4.4.3**).

4.4.2 Basic ideas

There are at least two motivations for seeking such a hybrid account. First, the two-factor theory and the prediction-error theory have different targets, and a hybrid account can be expected to explain both targets. The two-factor theory primarily aims to explain the delusions that can be monothematic and neuropsychological. The prediction-error theory, in contrast, primarily aims to explain delusions in the context of schizophrenia. A hybrid account can provide a unified explanation of both kinds of delusions.[16] Second, both the two-factor theory and the prediction-error theory have important theoretical and empirical merits, and a hybrid account can be expected to inherit the merits of both theories. The hybrid account, for instance, can be expected to be consistent with the empirical findings in support of the prediction-error theory, such as the finding in the allergy detection study by Corlett and colleagues (2007), and be able to offer the two-factor theoretic account of the dissociation cases, such as the case where people with vmPFC damage do not form the Capgras delusion.

A potential synthesis between the two-factor theory and the prediction-error theory has been discussed by several authors (e.g., Bortolotti & Miyazono, 2015; Coltheart, 2010; McKay, 2012; Miyazono et al., 2014).[17] In particular, Coltheart (2010) points out that what are regarded as the first factors in the two-factor theory often involve some expectations that are violated, i.e., prediction-errors. For example, the reduced autonomic response to familiar faces in the Capgras delusion could be regarded as a prediction-error, namely, a mismatch between the expected response and the actual autonomic response. Coltheart also suggests that the second factor has something to do with an abnormality in processing prediction-errors, in particular the kind of abnormality that was found in the allergy detection study by Corlett and colleagues (2007).

The hybrid theory inherits Coltheart's proposal and provides more details of the connection between the two-factor theory and the prediction-error theory. In the hybrid theory, the first/second factor distinction corresponds to a crucial distinction in the prediction-error framework, namely, the distinction between the prediction-error and its estimated precision. (The precision of a prediction-error is, roughly, an indicator of the trustworthiness of the prediction-error. See below for more.) The theory can be summarized as follows:

The hybrid account of delusion formation

There are two explanatory factors in the process of delusion formation. The first factor is some kind of misleading prediction-error, and the second factor is the observational adequacy bias that is driven by the overestimation of the precision of the prediction-error.

The hybrid theory inherits the idea, from the two-factor theory, that delusions are explained by two factors with different explanatory roles. The theme of a delusion is explained by the presence (and the nature) of the misleading prediction-error. The formation of the delusion is explained by the observational adequacy bias, which is driven by the overestimation of the precision of the prediction-error. The theory also inherits the insight, from the prediction-error theory, that delusions are caused by disturbances in the processing of mismatches between expectations and actual inputs. These disturbances, according to the hybrid theory, involve misleading prediction-errors (the first factor) and the overestimation of their precision (the second factor).

I will now explain the hybrid theory in detail.

The first factor: As Coltheart (2010) points out, the candidates for the first factor often involve some kind of prediction-error. For example, the reduced autonomic response to familiar faces in the case of the Capgras delusion involves the failed prediction of strong autonomic (or emotional) responses to familiar faces. Here are some other examples:

(1) The first factor of the delusion of mirrored-self misidentification (i.e., the delusion that one's reflection in the mirror is another person) in the case of F.E. (Breen, Cain, & Coltheart, 2001) has something to do with impaired face processing, which also involves a kind of prediction-error. As Coltheart (2007) notes, 'recognizing one's face in the mirror presumably is achieved by matching a face representation computed from what is seen in the mirror with a long-term stored representation of what one's face looks like in mirrors' (p. 1045). Although the image of his face in the mirror should have been perfectly familiar to F.E., impaired face processing may have produced a misleading mismatch between the actual input and the expected image derived from long-term representations.

(2) A failure of monitoring one's own actions is often regarded as the first factor of the delusion of alien control. Generally speaking, monitoring one's own actions can be understood as a predictive process in which a match between the expected sensory input and the actual sensory input serves as an indicator of a behavior being self-generated. In the case of the delusion of alien control, some abnormalities in the predictive process produce a misleading mismatch when a behavior is in fact self-generated, which results in failing to recognize the self-generatedness of the behavior (Fletcher & Frith, 2009; Frith & Friston, 2012).

(3) Referring to the prediction-error account of the delusion of reference, Coltheart (2010) suggests that the abnormal signaling of prediction-errors is the first factor of the delusion of reference. The abnormally signaled prediction-errors render the events and objects in the environment abnormally attention-grabbing or 'salient' (Kapur, 2003). When riding on a bus, for example, a person with the delusion of reference might find a pattern in the colors of the houses on a street. The pattern would not be very interesting for non-clinical individuals, but for this person it is abnormally salient due to the abnormally signaled prediction-errors:

> I sit on the top deck of the bus on the right hand side, looking out on the urban scene. But suddenly I notice a lot of the shops on the right hand side of the road are painted green. This strikes me as a definite pattern. I get up and move over to a window seat on the left. Then I notice that a lot on the left are painted red. It's red and green again! Always this red and green. They must have been painted that way recently by The Organisation. What are they trying to tell me?! It's a clue. It must be. I must work it out. Work out the meaning.
>
> (Chadwick, 2001, p. 53).

The abnormal salience of the pattern, in such a case, seems to be responsible for the theme of his delusion, namely that the pattern conveys some hidden meaning.

According to the hybrid theory, the first factor in the process of delusion formation is the presence of some kind of misleading prediction-error. The prediction-error is 'misleading' in the sense that it supports false representations of the world.[18] The presence of the misleading prediction-error is responsible for the theme of the delusion. For example, in the case of the Capgras delusion, the presence of the mismatch between the expected autonomic response and the actual autonomic response is responsible for the particular theme of the Capgras delusion (i.e., the idea that a familiar individual has been replaced by an imposter).

The second factor: As I have already indicated, there are different versions of the two-factor theory with different views about the nature of the second factor. Among others, the observational adequacy bias (or the discounting priors bias) is a plausible candidate for the second factor of many delusions. In the case of a person with the Capgras delusion about his wife, for example, the existing web of belief supports the hypothesis that the woman living in his house is his wife ('the wife hypothesis'), while the observational data from abnormal autonomic activities supports the hypothesis that she is an imposter ('the imposter hypothesis'). He accepts the imposter hypothesis because he prioritizes observational data over existing beliefs. On the other hand, a person with vmPFC damage might find himself in the same situation, where existing beliefs support the wife hypothesis and the observational data supports the imposter hypothesis. He does not accept the imposter hypothesis, however, because of the absence of the observational adequacy bias.

The observational adequacy bias, according to the hybrid theory, is the product of the overestimation of the precision of prediction-errors (e.g., Adams et al., 2013; Fletcher & Frith, 2009; Frith & Friston, 2012). In the prediction-error framework, prediction-errors are prioritized over prior beliefs when prediction-errors are estimated to be precise, while the prior beliefs are prioritized over prediction-errors when prediction-errors are estimated to be imprecise. The overestimation of precision, in this framework, results in the biased prioritizing of prediction-errors over prior beliefs.

According to the hybrid theory, the second factor in the delusion formation process is the observational adequacy bias, which is driven by the overestimation of precision. Prediction-errors that are in fact unreliable and misleading (the first factor) are misestimated as being highly precise (the second factor), and thus exert undue influence in the process of belief updating. The biased prioritizing of prediction-errors over prior beliefs is responsible for the formation of delusions. A man with the Capgras delusion, for example, might find himself in a situation in which his prior beliefs support the wife hypothesis, but in which misleading autonomic prediction-errors support the imposter hypothesis. He adopts the imposter hypothesis due to the biased prioritizing of misleading prediction-errors over prior beliefs. In contrast, a person with vmPFC damage, who is in the same situation but without the observational adequacy bias, might not adopt the imposter hypothesis.

4.4.3   *Advantages*

I will now describe the desirable features of the hybrid theory.

(1) The hybrid theory inherits theoretical and empirical merits from the two-factor theory and the prediction-error theory. The hybrid theory, just like the two-factor theory, provides a plausible account of the dissociation cases. For instance, people with vmPFC damage do not adopt the Capgras hypothesis despite the misleading autonomic prediction-error (first factor) because the misleading autonomic prediction-error is not sufficient for the adoption of the hypothesis. The adoption of the hypothesis also requires the observational adequacy bias, which is generated when the precision of the misleading prediction-error is overestimated.

The hybrid theory, just like the prediction-error theory, is consistent with the allergy detection study by Corlett and colleagues (2007) and other related studies (e.g., Corlett et al., 2006; Gradin et al., 2011; Murray et al., 2008). The allergy detection study might indicate the abnormal signaling of prediction-errors in schizophrenia, in which case the result of the study supports my hypothesis about the first factor (i.e., the first factor is the presence of misleading prediction-errors). Alternatively, the study might indicate the inappropriate processing of prediction-errors in schizophrenia, in which case the result supports my hypothesis about the second factor (i.e., the second factor is the observational adequacy bias due to the overestimation of precision).[19] Or, perhaps, the study indicates both the abnormal signaling of prediction-errors and the inappropriate processing of them in schizophrenia, in which case the result supports both hypotheses.

(2) The two-factor theory primarily aims to explain the delusions that can be monothematic and neuropsychological. The prediction-error theory, in contrast, primarily aims to explain delusions in the context of schizophrenia. The hybrid theory provides a unified explanation of both types of delusion.

That said, there could be some delusions about which we need to tell a slightly different story. The hybrid account explains delusions in terms of misleading prediction-errors and overestimating their precision. Overestimation of precision results in the misleading prediction-errors being prioritized over prior beliefs. This leads to the abnormal replacement of prior (true) beliefs with new false ones (what I will call 'Type-1 delusions'). Theoretically, there could also be some 'mirror image' cases of abnormal beliefs where some veridical prediction-errors ('veridical' in the sense that they support accurate representations of the world) are underestimated. Underestimation of precision would cause prior beliefs to be prioritized over veridical prediction-errors, resulting in a failure to replace prior beliefs that are no longer true with new true beliefs (what I will call 'Type-2 delusions').[20]

> *Type-1 delusions*: misleading prediction-error / overestimation of precision
>
> *Type-2 delusions*: veridical prediction-error / underestimation of precision

In many cases of delusion, what is remarkable is the fact that a person comes to believe a new and surprising hypothesis, such as the hypothesis that one's wife has been replaced by a Martian in disguise. These delusions nicely fit the model of Type-1 delusion; the person believes a new and surprising hypothesis because of the misleading prediction-error whose precision is overestimated.

However, in the case of anosognosia (i.e., the denial of illness), delusional hypotheses are typically neither new nor surprising. What is remarkable about anosognosia is that a person fails to revise an old and commonplace hypothesis (e.g., their left hand is not paralyzed) when it is evident that the hypothesis is no longer true (e.g., their left hand is obviously paralyzed after a stroke). The delusion in anosognosia does not fit very well with the model of Type-1 delusion, but it does fit the model of Type-2 delusion; the person fails to revise an old and commonplace hypothesis because of a veridical prediction-error whose precision is underestimated. For example, the paralysis caused by a stroke might produce prediction-errors such as the mismatches between the expected position and the actual position of the left hand when the person attempts to move it. They are veridical prediction-errors; they indicate something true about the world (e.g., the movement has not been properly executed). But if the precision of these veridical prediction-errors is underestimated, prior beliefs (i.e., the belief that the left hand is not paralyzed) will take precedence over the veridical prediction-errors, resulting in a failure to update the prior beliefs that are no longer true.[21]

The delusion in Reverse Othello syndrome might be another example of a Type-2 delusion. In the case reported by Butler (2000), which I mentioned Chapter 3, a man with Reverse Othello syndrome, after a serious car accident that caused severe head injury and quadriplegia, believed that his former romantic partner, who had severed all contact with him after the accident, still loved him despite obvious counterevidence.

Perhaps the delusion in Reverse Othello syndrome is similar to the delusion in anosognosia in some important respects. A remarkable feature in the case of anosognosia is the failure to revise prior beliefs that are no longer true. Similarly, a crucial feature in Butler's case seems to be the failure to revise the prior beliefs that are no longer true (e.g., the belief that his romantic partner loves him). Delusions in Reverse Othello syndrome might also be regarded as Type-2 delusions. For example, there are some unfulfilled expectations in Butler's case, such as the expectation that his partner would visit him in the hospital. These prediction-errors indicate something true about the world (i.e., she no longer loves him). But if the precision of these veridical prediction-errors is underestimated, prior beliefs will take precedence over the veridical prediction-errors, resulting in the failure to update the prior beliefs that are no longer true.

Strictly speaking, the delusion in Butler's case includes something more than what he had believed previously. For instance, his delusion that he and his former romantic partner married was not something he had believed before the accident. My hypothesis does not explain these types of delusions directly; they are not the result of the failure to update prior beliefs that are no longer true. I contend that these delusions are best regarded as the product of elaborating on the original delusional beliefs, and these original delusional beliefs are explained as the Type-2 delusion.

4.5 Summary

In this chapter, I have defended a two-factor theoretic account of the process of delusion formation. The two-factor theoretic framework is supported by the inference-to-the-best-explanation argument; the two-factor theory provides the best explanation of the important empirical and clinical observations.

I have also challenged the view, which is often expressed by the prediction-error theorists, that the two-factor theory and the prediction-error theory are alternative accounts to the process of delusion formation. These two theories do not have to be regarded as alternatives. I have shown that there could be a hybrid theory that incorporates the central ideas of the prediction-error theory into the (adoption) two-factor theoretic framework and that the hybrid theory has some desirable features. According to the hybrid theory, the first factor of a delusion is some misleading prediction-errors and the second factor is the observational adequacy bias due to an inappropriate estimation of the precision of the prediction-errors.

The hybrid theory is, thus, my answer to the etiology question. As I already noted in the beginning of this chapter, however, this answer is a tentative one because delusion formation is an open empirical issue. The hybrid theory is not presented as the complete account of the process of delusion formation but rather as a general theoretical framework that is supposed to be developed and modified in light of future empirical findings.

Notes

1 It is not my view that the two-factor theory and the prediction-error theory are the only available options. Certainly, there are other accounts that cannot be neglected; for example, see Bentall, Corcoran, Howard, Blackwood, and Kinderman (2001); Bentall, Kinderman, and Kaney (1994); Blakemore, Oakley, and Frith (2003); Freeman, Garety, Kuipers, Fowler, and Bebbington (2002); Frith (1992); Garety, Kuipers, Fowler, Freeman, and Bebbington (2001); Maher (1974).

2 The same thing is true for the prediction-error theory. I characterize the prediction-error theory in terms of its central theoretical commitments, rather than the details associated with some particular individuals. Just as in the case of the two-factor theory, there could be different versions of the prediction-error theory with different details.

3 'The first question is always: where did the delusion come from? – that is, what is responsible for the content of the delusional belief?' (Coltheart, 2007, p. 1044). I avoid the term 'content' because the first factor does not explain all the details of the content of the delusion. A person with the Capgras delusion might believe that his wife has been replaced by a Martian in disguise. The first factor (i.e., the abnormal data generated by reduced autonomic activities) does not explain all the details of this delusional belief. It does not explain why, for instance, he believes that his wife has been replaced by a Martian rather than a Venusian.

4 'The second question is always: why does the patient not reject the belief? (given that these beliefs are frequently bizarre, that there is good evidence that the belief is false, and that everyone around the patient will be denying that the belief is true) – that is, what is responsible for the persistence of the belief?' (Coltheart, 2007, p. 1044). I avoid the term 'persistence' or 'maintenance' because it rules out the adoption two-factor theory, according to which the second factor does the job of explaining the adoption (and the maintenance) of delusions.

5 But see also Gerrans (2000, 2002).

6 Similarly, the one-factor theorists can deny the reasonableness thesis. For example, they can maintain that adopting a delusional hypothesis is not reasonable but the second factor is not involved in the adoption process. Perhaps the unreasonable response to data is a general feature of the belief formation process. Gerrans makes the same point when he defends the one-factor account of the Cotard delusion; 'showing that a delusion depends on a systematic bias in reasoning that falls short of ideal standards of rationality is not sufficient to substantiate the two-stage account. The same type of reasoning biases are present in the general population' (2002). And Maher seems to suggest a view of this kind when he admits that people with delusions make irrational errors in reasoning tasks, such as the beads task (Huq et al., 1988), but insists that non-clinical people make similar errors (Maher, 2006).

7 However, Campbell (2001) defends 'rationalism' according to which the abnormal experience acquires its content by inheriting it from the delusion, which implies that, contrary to empiricism, the delusion exists before the abnormal experience. See Bayne and Pacherie (2004) for a response to Campbell's rationalism. See also Hohwy (2004) for a discussion of empiricism, rationalism, and the prediction-error theory.

8 But see Bell and colleagues (2017) for a discussion of the Capgras delusion and right hemisphere damages.

9 The jumping-to-conclusions bias, if it is causally relevant, seems to be coherent with the adoption two-factor theory; it explains why delusional hypotheses are adopted despite insufficient evidence. See, e.g., McKay (2012) and Stone and Young (1997).

10 The bias against disconfirmatory evidence, if it is causally relevant, seems to be coherent with the maintenance two-factor theory; it explains why delusional hypotheses are maintained despite the counterevidence available at the post-adoption stage. See, e.g., Moritz and colleagues (2017).

11 For example, Davies and colleagues (2001) argue that the jumping-to-conclusions bias cannot play the role of the second factor because it does not explain the maintenance of delusional hypotheses. Indeed, in the experiment by Huq and colleagues (1988), people with the jumping-to-conclusions bias required less evidence to adopt a hypothesis, but they also required less evidence to abandon the hypothesis in favor of another, which is inconsistent with the fact that people with delusions maintain delusional hypotheses despite overwhelming counterevidence.

12 See also Davies and Egan (2013), Parrott (2014), and Parrott and Koralus (2015).

13 But McKay adopts the phrase 'explanatory adequacy' rather than 'observational adequacy' (e.g., Aimola Davies & Davies, 2009).

14 This is similar to what van der Leer, Hartig, Goldmanis, and McKay (2015) claim about the jumping-to-conclusions bias; most people jump to conclusions, but delusion-prone people jump further.

15 See Griffiths, Langdon, Le Pelley, and Coltheart (2014) for a critical discussion of the studies by Corlett and colleagues. See Corlett and Fletcher (2015) for a response.
16 There are some exceptions. See, for example, Coltheart (2013) and Coltheart, Langdon, and McKay (2007) for a two-factor theoretic discussion of delusions in the context of schizophrenia, and Corlett and colleagues (2010) for a prediction-error theoretic discussion of the Capgras delusion, which can be monothematic and neuropsychological.
17 See also McKenna (2017).
18 Note that, on this formulation, the first factor in the delusion formation process could be, but need not be, the result of a brain abnormality.
19 Corlett and colleagues mention this possibility: 'it is perfectly possible that the rPFC is not the 'site' of prediction-error *per se* but may be concerned rather with inferences that are made as a consequence of prediction-error signal' (Corlett et al., 2007, p. 2397).
20 For a similar distinction, see Frith and Friston (2012).
21 The account of anosognosia by Frith and Friston (2012) is very similar to my account, except that, according to their view, it is the absence of veridical prediction-errors, rather than underestimating the precision of veridical precision-errors, that is responsible for the failure of updating prior beliefs.

References

Adams, R. A., Stephan, K. E., Brown, H. R., Frith, C. D., & Friston, K. J. (2013). The computational anatomy of psychosis. *Frontiers in Psychiatry*, *4*, 47.

Aimola Davies, A. M., & Davies, M. (2009). Explaining pathologies of belief. In M. R. Broome & L. Bortolotti (Eds.), *Psychiatry as cognitive neuroscience: Philosophical perspectives* (pp. 285–323). Oxford: Oxford University Press.

American Psychiatric Association. (2013). *Diagnostic and statistical manual of mental disorders* (5th ed.). Washington, DC: American Psychiatric Association.

Bayne, T., & Pacherie, E. (2004). Bottom-up or top-down: Campbell's rationalist account of monothematic delusions. *Philosophy, Psychiatry, & Psychology*, *11*(1), 1–11.

Bell, V., Marshall, C., Kanji, Z., Wilkinson, S., Halligan, P., & Deeley, Q. (2017). Uncovering Capgras delusion using a large-scale medical records database. *British Journal of Psychiatry Open*, *3*(4), 179–185.

Bentall, R. P., Corcoran, R., Howard, R., Blackwood, N., & Kinderman, P. (2001). Persecutory delusions: A review and theoretical integration. *Clinical Psychology Review*, *21*(8), 1143–1192.

Bentall, R. P., Kinderman, P., & Kaney, S. (1994). The self, attributional processes and abnormal beliefs: Towards a model of persecutory delusions. *Behaviour Research and Therapy*, *32*(3), 331–341.

Blakemore, S. J., Oakley, D. A., & Frith, C. D. (2003). Delusions of alien control in the normal brain. *Neuropsychologia*, *41*(8), 1058–1067.

Bortolotti, L., & Miyazono, K. (2015). Recent work on the nature and development of delusions. *Philosophy Compass*, *10*(9), 636–645.

Breen, N., Caine, D., & Coltheart, M. (2001). Mirrored-self misidentification: Two cases of focal onset dementia. *Neurocase*, *7*(3), 239–254.

Butler, P. V. (2000). Reverse Othello syndrome subsequent to traumatic brain injury. *Psychiatry, 63*(1), 85–92.

Campbell, J. (2001). Rationality, meaning, and the analysis of delusion. *Philosophy, Psychiatry, & Psychology, 8*(2), 89–100.

Chadwick, P. K. (2001). Psychotic consciousness. *International Journal of Social Psychiatry, 47*(1), 52–62.

Clark, A. (2013). Whatever next? Predictive brains, situated agents, and the future of cognitive science. *The Behavioral and Brain Sciences, 36*(3), 181–204.

Clark, A. (2016). *Surfing uncertainty: Prediction, action, and the embodied mind.* New York, NY: Oxford University Press.

Coltheart, M. (2007). The 33rd Sir Frederick Bartlett Lecture: Cognitive neuropsychiatry and delusional belief. *The Quarterly Journal of Experimental Psychology, 60*(8), 1041–1062.

Coltheart, M. (2010). The neuropsychology of delusions. *Annals of the New York Academy of Sciences, 1191*(1), 16–26.

Coltheart, M. (2013). On the distinction between monothematic and polythematic delusions. *Mind & Language, 28*(1), 103–112.

Coltheart, M., Langdon, R., & McKay, R. (2007). Schizophrenia and monothematic delusions. *Schizophrenia Bulletin, 33*(3), 642–647.

Coltheart, M., Langdon, R., & McKay, R. (2011). Delusional belief. *Annual Review of Psychology, 62*, 271–298.

Coltheart, M., Menzies, P., & Sutton, J. (2010). Abductive inference and delusional belief. *Cognitive Neuropsychiatry, 15*(1–3), 261–287.

Corcoran, R., Cummins, S., Rowse, G., Moore, R., Blackwood, N., Howard, R., . . . & Bentall, R. P. (2006). Reasoning under uncertainty: Heuristic judgments in patients with persecutory delusions or depression. *Psychological Medicine, 36*(8), 1109–1118.

Corlett, P. R., & Fletcher, P. C. (2015). Delusions and prediction error: Clarifying the roles of behavioural and brain responses. *Cognitive Neuropsychiatry, 20*(2), 95–105.

Corlett, P. R., Aitken, M. R., Dickinson, A., Shanks, D. R., Honey, G. D., Honey, R. A., . . . & Fletcher, P. C. (2004). Prediction error during retrospective revaluation of causal associations in humans: fMRI evidence in favor of an associative model of learning. *Neuron, 44*(5), 877–888.

Corlett, P. R., Honey, G. D., Aitken, M. R., Dickinson, A., Shanks, D. R., Absalom, A. R., . . . & Robbins, T. W. (2006). Frontal responses during learning predict vulnerability to the psychotogenic effects of ketamine: Linking cognition, brain activity, and psychosis. *Archives of General Psychiatry, 63*(6), 611–621.

Corlett, P. R., Honey, G. D., & Fletcher, P. C. (2016). Prediction error, ketamine and psychosis: An updated model. *Journal of Psychopharmacology, 30*(11), 1145–1155.

Corlett, P. R., Krystal, J. H., Taylor, J. R., & Fletcher, P. C. (2009). Why do delusions persist? *Frontiers in Human Neuroscience, 3*, 12.

Corlett, P. R., Murray, G., Honey, G., Aitken, M., Shanks, D., Robbins, T., . . . & Fletcher, P. (2007). Disrupted prediction-error signal in psychosis: Evidence for an associative account of delusions. *Brain, 130*(9), 2387–2400.

Corlett, P. R., Taylor, J. R., Wang, X. J., Fletcher, P. C., & Krystal, J. H. (2010). Toward a neurobiology of delusions. *Progress in Neurobiology, 92*(3), 345–369.

Davies, M., Coltheart, M., Langdon, R., & Breen, N. (2001). Monothematic delusions: Towards a two-factor account. *Philosophy, Psychiatry, & Psychology, 8*(2), 133–158.

Davies, M., & Egan, A. (2013). Delusion: Cognitive approaches Bayesian inference and compartmentalisation. In K. W. M. Fulford, M. Davies, R. G. T. Gipps, & G. Graham (Eds.), *Oxford handbook of philosophy and psychiatry* (pp. 689–727). Oxford: Oxford University Press.

Ellis, H. D., & Young, A. W. (1990). Accounting for delusional misidentifications. *The British Journal of Psychiatry, 157*(2), 239–248.

Fletcher, P. C., & Frith, C. D. (2009). Perceiving is believing: a Bayesian approach to explaining the positive symptoms of schizophrenia. *Nature Reviews Neuroscience, 10*(1), 48–58.

Freeman, D., Garety, P. A., Kuipers, E., Fowler, D., & Bebbington, P. E. (2002). A cognitive model of persecutory delusions. *British Journal of Clinical Psychology, 41*(4), 331–347.

Friston, K. (2005). A theory of cortical responses. *Philosophical Transactions of the Royal Society B: Biological Sciences, 360*(1456), 815–836.

Friston, K. (2010). The free-energy principle: A unified brain theory? *Nature Reviews Neuroscience, 11*(2), 127.

Frith, C. (1992). *The cognitive neuropsychology of schizophrenia.* Hove: Psychology Press.

Frith, C. D., & Friston, K. J. (2012). False perceptions and false beliefs: Understanding schizophrenia. In A. M. Battro, S. Dehaene, M. S. Sorondo, & W. J. Singer (Eds.), *The proceedings of the working group on neurosciences and the human person: New perspectives on human activities* (pp. 134–148). Vatican City: The Pontifical Academy of Sciences.

Garety, P. A., Kuipers, E., Fowler, D., Freeman, D., & Bebbington, P. E. (2001). A cognitive model of the positive symptoms of psychosis. *Psychological Medicine, 31*(2), 189–195.

Gerrans, P. (2000). Refining the explanation of Cotard's delusion. *Mind & Language, 15*(1), 111–122.

Gerrans, P. (2002). A one-stage explanation of the Cotard delusion. *Philosophy, Psychiatry, & Psychology, 9*(1), 47–53.

Gradin, V. B., Kumar, P., Waiter, G., Ahearn, T., Stickle, C., Milders, M., . . . & Steele, J. D. (2011). Expected value and prediction error abnormalities in depression and schizophrenia. *Brain, 134*(6), 1751–1764.

Griffiths, O., Langdon, R., Le Pelley, M. E., & Coltheart, M. (2014). Delusions and prediction error: Re-examining the behavioural evidence for disrupted error signalling in delusion formation. *Cognitive Neuropsychiatry, 19*(5), 439–467.

Hohwy, J. (2004). Top-down and bottom-up in delusion formation. *Philosophy, Psychiatry, & Psychology, 11*(1), 65–70.

Hohwy, J. (2013). *The predictive mind.* New York, NY: Oxford University Press.

Hohwy, J., & Rosenberg, R. (2005). Unusual experiences, reality testing and delusions of alien control. *Mind & Language, 20*(2), 141–162.

Huq, S. F., Garety, P. A., & Hemsley, D. R. (1988). Probabilistic judgements in deluded and non-deluded subjects. *The Quarterly Journal of Experimental Psychology, 40*(4), 801–812.

Kahneman, D., & Tversky, A. (1973). On the psychology of prediction. *Psychological Review*, *80*(4), 237–251.

Kapur, S. (2003). Psychosis as a state of aberrant salience: A framework linking biology, phenomenology, and pharmacology in schizophrenia. *American Journal of Psychiatry*, *160*(1), 13–23.

Leitgeb, H. (2017). *The stability of belief: How rational belief coheres with probability*. New York, NY: Oxford University Press.

Maher, B. A. (1974). Delusional thinking and perceptual disorder. *Journal of Individual Psychology*, *30*(1), 98–113.

Maher, B. A. (2006). The relationship between delusions and hallucinations. *Current Psychiatry Reports*, *8*(3), 179–183.

McKay, R. (2012). Delusional inference. *Mind & Language*, *27*(3), 330–355.

McKenna, P. (2017). *Delusions: Understanding the un-understandable*. Cambridge: Cambridge University Press.

Miyazono, K., Bortolotti, L., & Broome, M. R. (2014). Prediction-error and two-factor theories of delusion formation. In N. Galbraith (Ed.), *Aberrant beliefs and reasoning* (pp. 34–54). Hove: Psychology Press.

Moritz, S., Pfuhl, G., Lüdtke, T., Menon, M., Balzan, R. P., & Andreou, C. (2017). A two-stage cognitive theory of the positive symptoms of psychosis. Highlighting the role of lowered decision thresholds. *Journal of Behavior Therapy and Experimental Psychiatry*, *56*, 12–20.

Moritz, S., & Woodward, T. S. (2006). A generalized bias against disconfirmatory evidence in schizophrenia. *Psychiatry Research*, *142*(2), 157–165.

Murray, G. K., Corlett, P. R., Clark, L., Pessiglione, M., Blackwell, A. D., Honey, G., . . . & Fletcher, P. C. (2008). Substantia nigra/ventral tegmental reward prediction error disruption in psychosis. *Molecular Psychiatry*, *13*(3), 267.

Parrott, M. (2014). Bayesian models, delusional beliefs, and epistemic possibilities. *The British Journal for the Philosophy of Science*, *67*(1), 271–296.

Parrott, M., & Koralus, P. (2015). The erotetic theory of delusional thinking. *Cognitive Neuropsychiatry*, *20*(5), 398–415.

Reimer, M. (2009). Is the impostor hypothesis really so preposterous? Understanding the Capgras experience. *Philosophical Psychology*, *22*(6), 669–686.

Stone, T., & Young, A. W. (1997). Delusions and brain injury: The philosophy and psychology of belief. *Mind & Language*, *12*(3–4), 327–364.

Tranel, D., Damasio, H., & Damasio, A. R. (1995). Double dissociation between overt and covert face recognition. *Journal of Cognitive Neuroscience*, *7*(4), 425–432.

Van der Leer, L., Hartig, B., Goldmanis, M., & McKay, R. (2015). Delusion proneness and "jumping to conclusions": Relative and absolute effects. *Psychological Medicine*, *45*(6), 1253–1262.

Woodward, T. S., Moritz, S., Cuttler, C., & Whitman, J. C. (2006). The contribution of a cognitive Bias Against Disconfirmatory Evidence (BADE) to delusions in schizophrenia. *Journal of Clinical and Experimental Neuropsychology*, *28*(4), 605–617.

Young, A. W., Leafhead, K. M., & Szulecka, K. (1994). The Capgras and Cotard delusions. *Psychopathology*, *27*(3–5), 226–231.

Conclusion
A biological account of delusions

In this book, I defended the malfunctional belief hypothesis, according to which delusions are malfunctional beliefs. Just like non-delusional beliefs, delusions have doxastic functions and, hence, they belong to the category of belief. This is my answer to the nature question (**Chapter 2**). Unlike non-delusional beliefs, however, delusions are malfunctional; they directly or indirectly involve some cognitive mechanisms that fail to perform their functions due to intrinsic problems. Delusions are pathological mental states because they are malfunctional and they have significant negative impacts on well-being. This is my answer to the pathology question (**Chapter 3**). And the malfunctional belief hypothesis is coherent with the hybrid account of delusion formation, which combines the basic ideas of two leading theories of delusion formation, namely, the two-factor theory and the prediction-error theory. The hybrid theory is my answer to the etiology question (**Chapter 4**).

Teleo-functionalism, which provides the theoretical foundation of my arguments in this book, emphasizes the analogy between internal organ categories, such as the category of heart, and mental state categories, such as the category of belief. The category of heart might be defined in terms of the function of pumping blood; something is a heart if and only if it has the function of pumping blood. Similarly, the category of belief might be defined in terms of doxastic functions; something is a belief if and only if it has doxastic functions. And this analogy is related to another crucial analogy in this book, namely, the analogy between the disordered internal organs, such as disordered hearts, and the disordered mental states, such as delusions. A disordered heart fails to perform the function of pumping blood (or some other functions, e.g., some tissue-level functions in the case of pericarditis), and the failure has negative impacts on well-being. Similarly, a delusional belief fails to perform doxastic functions (or, more precisely, some cognitive mechanisms that are directly or indirectly related to the delusional belief fail to perform their functions due to intrinsic problems), and the failure has negative impacts on well-being.

My account of belief is a biological one; just like the category of heart, the category of belief is defined biologically, in terms of biological or etiological functions. My account of delusion is also a biological one; just like disordered hearts, delusional beliefs are explained biologically, in terms of biological or etiological malfunction. But, if my account of delusion is biological, does the account imply that a delusion is a disorder of the brain (or a symptom of a brain disorder)?

What is meant by the claim that a mental disorder (or a symptom of it) is a brain disorder? An interpretation is that it means a form of reductionism, which has an 'optimistic take on the success of reducing psychiatry to neurobiology, and views psychiatric disorders as being validated through the discovery of a discrete, identifiable biological "essence"' (Broome & Bortolotti, 2009, p. 25).[1]

In the context of psychiatry, the term 'biological' often means 'physical', 'neurological', or 'organic'. For example, 'biological psychiatry' typically means 'neuroscientific psychiatry' or 'psychiatric neuroscience'. According to this usage of the term, 'biological account' might mean 'reductionist account'. But this is not my usage of the term 'biological'.[2] In my usage, 'biological account' means 'evolutionary account'. For example, an evolutionary psychological approach to mind and behavior can be described as a 'biological' approach, but it might not be a reductionist approach. (But I do not rule out the possibility that some evolutionary psychological approaches are reductionist approaches in fact. My claim is just that an evolutionary psychological approach does not have to be a reductionist approach.) An evolutionary psychological approach is 'biological' not because it involves reductionism but because it explains mind and behavior in terms of the biological processes, including natural selection, that are responsible for the production of biological traits in general.

A philosophical objection is that if a mental state is a product of the biological processes (the process of natural selection in particular), then it is identical with a neurological state. Hence, 'evolutionary' implies 'reductionist' anyway. The argument might go as follows. If a mental state S is a product of natural selection, then S enhances biological fitness. And if S enhances biological fitness, then S is causally efficacious. (Otherwise, S cannot have any causal consequences, including the consequence of enhancing biological fitness.) Therefore, if S is a product of natural selection, then S is causally efficacious. Now, assuming the causal exclusion argument (e.g., Kim, 2000), if S is causally efficacious (and if S's physical effects are not causally overdetermined), then S is identical with a neurological state N. Putting these arguments together, if S is a product of natural selection, then it is identical with N.

I will not discuss this objection here because the objection will take us too far away from the main topic of this book. In any case, it is clear that teleo-functionalism is a non-reductionist account. After all, teleo-functionalism is a form of functionalism, and it is the fundamental feature functionalism that it opposes reductionism. Thus, my teleo-functionalist account of delusion does not imply that a delusion is reducible to a disordered brain state. But here is a related question. Certainly, functionalism denies that a mental state is reducible to a neurological state, but it does not deny that a mental state has a physical basis. In particular, it does not deny that a mental state is physically realized by a neurological state. But, then, does my account imply that a delusion is physically realized by a disordered brain state?

My answer to this question is 'No'; my account does not imply that a delusion is physically realized by a disordered brain state. (Please note that I am not saying that my account implies that a delusion is not physically realized by a disordered brain state.)

Functionalism is often characterized with the software–hardware analogy: Mental states are software states and brain states are hardware states. Teleo-functionalism is also committed to this analogy (although it emphasizes the biological aspect of the 'software' and the 'hardware'). As Papineau (1994) points out, a computer can have a software problem without a hardware problem:

> Now suppose that there is some bug in the program [of MS word 5.0]. For example, suppose that whenever either of us tries to double-space a highlighted section, that section gets deleted. (This is just for the sake of the argument: I've never found this or any other bug in MS Word 5.0.) This obviously wouldn't show that there was anything physically wrong with out [sic] machines. It would be silly to get the hardware engineer to come and solve the problem. The logic circuits are all working as they are supposed to. Rather, the fault lies entirely at the software level.
>
> (p. 79)

For the same reason, according to functionalism (including teleo-functionalism), someone can develop what Papineau calls a 'pure mental disorder', namely, a mental disorder without a brain disorder.

An objection is that the software–hardware analogy is not strong. Certainly, it is absurd to fix the hardware in order to fix a software problem. But it is not so absurd to 'fix' the brain (e.g., by pharmaceutical interventions) in order to treat a mental disorder. However, this objection can be answered. After all, the same thing is true, at least to some degree, about software problems. There are some physical things one can do to the hardware in order to alleviate some software problems (e.g., turning it off and waiting for a while, cooling it, etc.), but this does not mean that the problems are in fact hardware problems. Similarly, there are certainly some physical things one can do to the brain in order to alleviate some (symptoms of) mental disorders, but this does not mean that the mental disorders are in fact brain disorders.

I endorse Papineau's claim that, according to functionalism (including teleo-functionalism), there can be a disordered mental state without a disordered neurological state (or, there can be a disordered mental state that is not realized by a disordered neurological state). But, functionalism only allows for the theoretical possibility of a disordered mental state without a disordered neurological state. It is an empirical matter whether there is in fact a disordered mental state without a disordered neurological state.

It is an empirical matter whether there is in fact a delusion without a disordered neurological state. Of course, it is very likely that neuropsychological delusions involve disordered neurological states. The open question is whether non-neuropsychological delusions involve disordered neurological states.

It should be noted that the idea of a delusion without a disordered neurological state is perfectly consistent with some neurological differences (including structural differences and functional differences) between the group of people with delusions and the group of non-clinical people. 'Neurological difference' does not necessarily mean 'neurological disorder'. There might be some neurological differences between the group of people with a very high IQ and the group of people with an average IQ, but it does not necessary mean that people in the former group have a neurological disorder (although some of them might have a neurological disorder).

The neurological differences between the delusional group and the non-clinical group are expectable without sophisticated empirical investigations; it simply follows from physicalism that there should be such differences. There is an obvious mental difference between a person, A, who is in the delusional group and a person, B, who in the non-clinical group; A has delusional beliefs, but B does not. And the mind–body supervenience thesis (except for the 'global' supervenience; e.g., Haugeland, 1984), which is accepted by many philosophers as the minimal commitment of physicalism, implies that there are some neurological differences between A and B. In contrast, it does not simply follow from physicalism that A has a neurological disorder.

In sum, my teleo-functionalist account of belief is biological; the category of belief is analogous to the category of heart. And my account of delusion is biological, too; delusional beliefs are analogous to disordered hearts. But this does not imply that a delusion is reducible to a brain disorder. In fact, teleo-functionalism is a non-reductionist account. In addition, teleo-functionalism allows for the theoretical possibility that a delusion is a disordered mental state without a disordered neurological state.

Notes

1 Alternatively, it might mean a form of eliminativism, according to which 'if the entities of psychiatry cannot be reduced to their putative biological underpinnings, and psychiatry cannot be successfully reduced to neuroscience, then psychiatric classification is not useful and will be gradually replaced by neurological classification' (Broome & Bortolotti, 2009, p. 25).
2 When 'biological' is contrasted with 'environmental', 'cultural', or 'social', it means 'genetic' or 'innate'. But this is not my usage, either.

References

Broome, M. R., & Bortolotti, L. (2009). Mental illness as mental: In defence of psychological realism. *Humana.Mente*, *11*, 25–43.
Haugeland, J. (1984). Ontological supervenience. *The Southern Journal of Philosophy*, *22*(S1), 1–12.
Kim, J. (2000). *Mind in a physical world: An essay on the mind-body problem and mental causation*. Cambridge, MA: The MIT Press.
Papineau, D. (1994). Mental disorder, illness and biological disfunction. *Royal Institute of Philosophy Supplements*, *37*, 73–82.

Index

For Product Safety Concerns and Information please contact our EU representative GPSR@taylorandfrancis.com Taylor & Francis Verlag GmbH, Kaufingerstraße 24, 80331 München, Germany

Batch number: 08153772

Printed by Printforce, the Netherlands